Michael Angulo

TODAY'S EVANGELISM: COUNTERFEIT OR GENUINE?

Gordon H. Clark

The Trinity Foundation
Jefferson, Maryland

Today's Evangelism: Counterfeit or Genuine?
© 1990 The Trinity Foundation
Post Office Box 700
Jefferson, Maryland 21755
Printed in the United States of America.
ISBN: 0-940931-28-1

Contents

Books by Gordon H. Clark

Readings in Ethics (1931)
Selections from Hellenistic Philosophy (1940)
A History of Philosophy (coauthor, 1941)
A Christian Philosophy of Education (1946, 1988)
A Christian View of Men and Things (1952)
What Presbyterians Believe (1956)[1]
Thales to Dewey (1957, 1989)
Dewey (1960)
Religion, Reason and Revelation (1961, 1986)
William James (1963)
Karl Barth's Theological Method (1963)
The Philosophy of Science and Belief in God (1964, 1987)
What Do Presbyterians Believe? (1965, 1985)
Peter Speaks Today (1967)[2]
The Philosophy of Gordon H. Clark (1968)
Biblical Predestination (1969)[3]
Historiography: Secular and Religious (1971)
II Peter (1972)[2]
The Johannine Logos (1972, 1989)
Three Types of Religious Philosophy (1973, 1989)
First Corinthians (1975)
Colossians (1979, 1989)
Predestination in the Old Testament (1979)[3]
I and II Peter (1980)
Language and Theology (1980)
First John (1980)
God's Hammer: The Bible and Its Critics (1982, 1987)
Behaviorism and Christianity (1982)
Faith and Saving Faith (1983, 1990)
In Defense of Theology (1984)
The Pastoral Epistles (1984)
The Biblical Doctrine of Man (1984)
The Trinity (1985)
Logic (1985, 1988)
Ephesians (1985)
Clark Speaks From the Grave (1986)
Logical Criticisms of Textual Criticism (1986)
First and Second Thessalonians (1986)
Predestination (1987)
The Atonement (1987)
The Incarnation (1988)
Today's Evangelism: Counterfeit or Genuine? (1990)

[1] Revised in 1965 as *What Do Presbyterians Believe?*
[2] Combined in 1980 as *I & II Peter.*
[3] Combined in 1987 as *Predestination.*

Foreword

One of the sins for which Christ condemned the scribes and Pharisees—the religious leaders of his day—was their dynamic evangelistic program.

> Woe to you, scribes and Pharisees, hypocrites! For you travel land and sea to win one proselyte, and when he is won, you make him twice as much a son of hell as yourselves.

Synagogue growth—church growth—making converts—is not enough. The important question is: To what are the listeners being converted? What is the message that is being taught and believed?

The central issue in today's—and yesterday's—evangelism is not the method, but the message, although the message will shape the method. The evangelistic program of the scribes and Pharisees was apparently large, dynamic, and effective—yet it was making sons of hell. At the end of the twentieth century religious organizations, both church and para-church, some of them highly respected, operate similarly extensive and successful evangelistic programs, and the result is the same. They are making millions children of hell.

The message, the teaching, the doctrine of the evangelist is what separates genuine Christian evangelism from counterfeit evangelism. It is not only the recognized cults that have perverted the Gospel, but most of the historically Christian churches as well. If a cult be defined as a religious group that finds its authority in something besides the Bible—whether it be the *Book of Mormon, Science and Health with a Key to the Scriptures,* the *Koran,* the *ex cathedra* pronouncements of the Bishop of Rome, or the leadings of the "Spirit," then virtually all American religious organizations are cults. All of these cults are concerned about growth, just as the scribes and Pharisees were. But the concern and the focus of the Christian evangelist is not growth, but truth, and if that truth is preached clearly, "the Lord [will] add to the church daily those who [are] being saved," and they will "[continue] steadfastly in the apostles' doctrine. . . ." Growth, as a goal, is the ideology of the cancer cell. True evangelism has a different goal: the propagation of God's truth. If the Gospel is preached to every creature, God will convert all his people, all he has chosen for heaven.

John W. Robbins
June 9, 1990

Chapter One

Introduction

When a congregation and its pastor decide to pay special attention to evangelism, they may invite a recommended speaker, set aside two weeks for meetings, and scatter advertisements around the neighborhood. But there is a great deal more to evangelism than this. One must ask, What kind of man is the recommended evangelist? What kind of music will he introduce? What kind of sermon does he preach? What will be the tone of the meetings? There are also other questions. What preparations should the church make before the evangelist comes? What sort of follow-up should be scheduled for the week after the evangelist leaves? And this last question points out the fact that evangelism is not limited to special meetings with special speakers. If a pastor and congregation wish to pay attention to evangelism, they may conclude that evangelism is a year-round affair, and possibly they may finally decide that an outside speaker is not so important after all. The pastor himself may be more important. And the ordinary members of the congregation may be the most important of all. These are points that the following pages will consider.

Evangelism is an indispensable part of a church's program because evangelism is an indispensable part of the Church's program. If the Church does not continually win people to Christ, the Church will die. And it looks as if the Church were dying. Many denominations are not keeping up with the growth of the population in the West. The growth of the population in the East gives a still more pessimistic picture. In the times of the Apostles, the Lord added to the Church daily those who were being saved. This occurred daily. How many local congregations can say that they add new members daily? There may be some, but I do not happen to know where they are. Most churches do not have large increases. And in many cases, increases do not mean that people are coming to accept Christ. It may merely mean that many people are moving to the suburbs, so that the suburban churches grow, while the downtown churches die. It may also mean that the particular congregation is an efficient country club, or political action group, having nothing to do with apostolic Christianity. Growth is not necessarily evangelism.

What is the cause of the present evil days? Is it personal sin on the part of the church members that hinders growth? Maybe it is. Is it the pressure of secular society in this post-Christian age that blocks out the message from people's minds? Maybe it is. Is it because the message is not preached? Well, that is often the case too. Or again, is it because God had planned a great apostasy at the end of the age, and now that that time has arrived God is blinding the minds of the people so that hearing they do not hear? This could be so too.

Nevertheless, God's command still rests on us to preach the Gospel to every creature. The Church always has been and always will be a minority group in this world; its numbers may be decreasing at the present time; but the Church must not die, it will not die. The present members will all die in a few years, if the Lord does not soon return, and new members must be sought. They will be sought. They will be found. God will not permit his Church to be extinguished. Now, our question is, How may we preserve the Church? God will preserve the Church, but only through the efforts of his servants. It is we who must do the work. Evangelism is indispensable. Somehow the Church must gather in new people.

Somehow; but how? There are many methods in actual use. Surely some are better than others. Since the problem is serious and important, careful thought should be given to how evangelization should be conducted. Some methods may be good in one situation and bad in another. Some may do more harm than good. Bingo is one of these. No, if a church wants to pay attention to evangelism, it should not thoughtlessly plunge ahead. It must face the questions that different methods pose, carefully consider the probable effects, and then choose deliberately what the situation requires. Too often inertia produces an automatic acceptance of customary procedures. Evangelistic services have become stereotyped. They all follow the same form. Happy singing, impassioned address, altar call with pleading, shaking hands, signing cards, love offering, and good-bye till the next campaign. Well, once in a while the form should be scrutinized. If it is a good method, it will survive scrutiny. If it has weak spots, it can be improved. And if it is unbiblical, it should be scrapped. Since these are dark days for the Church, it is all the more important to examine the whole procedure now. It is all the more reprehensible to react automatically and go through some familiar motions. Evangelism requires very serious consideration.

There are all too many points at which this study could begin. The one chosen here has to do with the *tone* of the evangelistic service. We shall examine the place of emotion in evangelism. This matter is really more important than it may at first seem. It brings to light elements of great significance in the life of the church that holds these services. As the discussion continues, some readers may think that we are getting bogged down in trivialities. We shall indeed examine many details, but they have a real bearing on our efforts to bring people to Christ.

Since the subject is so important, and the need in this age so great, it pays to take time to examine a good many details.

Furthermore, the place of emotion in evangelism is suitable for beginning this study because it covers all phases of the work. It is a matter of disagreement, since, as all can see, the various churches differ in the degrees of emotion and excitement, or the lack of them, the style of the music, and the type of prayer that characterize their conduct. Surely among all these differences, some are better than others. Which? Let me give an initial example of a funeral service. Funerals are not generally considered evangelistic occasions. But some groups definitely turn a funeral into an evangelistic appeal. Others think that this is the depth of poor taste. The Church may indeed be under God's order to evangelize. But it is also under God's order to comfort those who mourn. This latter should not be neglected, even in favor of the former. At any rate, let me tell you about a funeral.

When I was a graduate student, a highly respected professor suddenly died of ptomaine poisoning. A number of students attended the funeral in a nearby Episcopal church. I had never been to an Episcopal funeral before. The funerals I had attended included some remarks about the decedent. The eulogy might be too fulsome. It might be more restrained. But some memories of the person's life and activity were mentioned. Most of the funerals I had attended were in very good taste; sickening sweet, not to say deceptive eulogies, were avoided. But at this Episcopal service the minister read from the prayer book and said nothing whatever about our beloved professor. I thought the service cold and forbidding. But later the widow, whom most of us knew fairly well because the professor held his classes in his home, served coffee and remarked how comforting and beautiful the service was. Naturally, I did not want to hurt her by telling her my own feelings; but I could not help being struck by the difference in the effect that funeral had on me and its effect on her. Obviously a given type of service does not have the same effect on all people. And this is true of evangelistic services as well.

Now, let me tell you about an evangelistic service. The evangelist had his wife and children on the stage with him. Stage? Well, it was quite a show. Each child played some instrument—a saw, a queer stringed instrument, a bass wash tub, and the wife played the piano. Everybody was whooping it up. When everyone was in a good mood, the pastor announced the offering. Not enough money was collected the first time, and after the pastor explained how costly it was to educate several children, who stood grinning on the stage, the plates were passed again. I forget whether they were passed a third time, for it was already nine-thirty, and I thought I had better leave.

In some of these pentecostal meetings the people speak in tongues. They yell and rant and rave. They fall on the floor. One friend of mine remarked that in the Bible people sometimes fell on their faces, but in these meetings the women fell on their backs, face up. Well, this is hardly an Episcopal funeral.

Now, for another example. During our summer vacations, when we travel widely in the West, it is a problem to know where to attend church on the Lord's Day. The larger denominations are sunk in various degrees of apostasy, and we think it useless even to hope for a really Christian service. The smaller denominations and independent churches may actually profess to believe the Bible, but their interpretation of it can be somewhat bizarre, and their "tone" is unpredictable. We have found that the Missouri Synod Lutheran Churches are the best choice in these unfamiliar localities. They uniformly have good sermons. No one throws a fit; and if the German music is sometimes too high to sing in comfort, at least it is good music and the themes are Biblical. I remember an excellent service in Yosemite National Park, another in Reno, and one nearer home on Route 30 just east of Warsaw, Indiana. Here the pastor spent a few minutes referring to America's contemporary orgy of sex. With restrained force, which made it all the more forceful, he earnestly declared that sex is perfectly all right in its place, and its place is in marriage, and nowhere else.

But this was not an evangelistic service. Or was it? As a Christian I was impressed by the sermon. Had I not been a Christian, I think I still would have been impressed. If people are to be turned from their sins to seek Christ, must they not be convinced of their sins? Then must not preaching the Ten Commandments be a part of the evangelistic endeavor? Because that Lutheran service was dignified, even formal, was it therefore not evangelistic? Maybe it was the very best kind of evangelism. Before we judge, we shall have to decide what evangelism really is. That is another point that must be discussed.

We do agree, do we not, that evangelism has something to do with preaching the Gospel? If so, then some of the Quaker services, in which everybody sits silent and no one says a word, cannot be evangelistic services. Here the "tone" of the service precludes evangelism. This is one extreme. The tones mentioned have ranged from the absolute silence, through an Episcopal funeral service, all the way to screaming in unknown tongues and falling on the floor unconscious. Obviously, before a pastor and a congregation engage in two weeks of actual services, they must have some notion of what sort of tone they intend to develop.

This matter of the range of tone can be summarized as a question of the degree of emotion produced or aimed at in these services. Not only is the degree of emotion to be considered, but also the quality of the emotion. There are various emotions.

Should the evangelist try to stimulate and play on all emotions? Should he try for one or two only? And if so, which ones? Let us also keep in mind that these questions are pertinent, not only for the planning of evangelistic services, but also for regular, ordinary worship services as well. More than that, those questions apply to our individual activities, our personal devotions, our mode of life. Above it was hinted that evangelism may not be solely the province of an itinerant evangelist. The pastor must evangelize. And has not God laid the obligation to evangelize on every Christian? In that case each of us must consider the tone of his life as it affects his witness to Christ. No doubt there is also much else to be considered. This is only the first point, for we have to begin the discussion somewhere. The last point—well, we shall never get to the last point. There are too many for this small book.

The best way to conclude this introductory chapter is to indicate the method by which all these questions can be answered. Observation of many evangelistic campaigns and an evaluation of their results is not, not, I say, the method of deciding what to do and how to do it. If one had lived long enough, one could have attended Moody's meetings, Billy Sunday's, and Billy Graham's. In them one could observe the music. Billy Sunday, actually Rodeheaver, used a klaxon horn with that grand old hymn of the Church, *The Brewer's Big Hosses Can't Run Over Me.* He also used sawdust. In fact, Billy Sunday had a remarkable grasp of acoustics, and, with the exception of that piece of scalloped wood that hung over his head like the sword of Damocles, he could hardly be improved upon in those days before public address systems. Now, attention to acoustics is not to be despised; but this is not the way to evaluate the evangelistic results.

One popular way of evaluating evangelistic campaigns is to count the number of people who attended. The counting is not always correct. Evangelists as a group have made a bad name for themselves by their overestimates of the attendance. Just this past week I read a religious paper which said "400 were present— evangelistically speaking 600." But aside from the question as to whether the number is correctly counted or not, the number is no indication of success. Sports regularly outdraw church services. Does not the World Series attract some fifty thousand each game? What matters is not how many people are present, but what is done. An evangelistic endeavor that reaches only one person may be a more successful endeavor than one where a thousand people are present. Statistics cannot measure Christian value.

Of course there is one difference between the World Series and an evangelistic campaign. In the former no one comes forward. They all go home after the game. In the evangelistic service one can count the number who come forward at the invitation; and some people think that this is the way to measure the evangelist's success. But of the twenty signed cards transmitted to our church at the end of a Graham campaign, nineteen addresses had no such person living there, and the one boy we found had not the slightest idea of what the card was supposed to mean. Maybe the evangelist had done these people some good, but our church was unable to find what good had been done.

At the end of the Billy Sunday campaign in 1915 our church received into its membership over a hundred persons. I myself was one of them. Another was a streetcar conductor who wanted to take over the Sabbath morning worship service to describe his enthusiastic emotional experiences. Two others were a man and wife who put away their whiskey and remained sober, faithful members for the rest of their lives. Now, I do not mean to be antagonistic to Billy Sunday. I believe he really did some good. But I know that had he not come to town, I would have nonetheless professed faith in Christ and become a church member. Maybe the couple who put away their liquor were actually converted by means of Sunday's sermons. Whether the conductor was converted, I do not know. He did not last long. But all the observable results are of no use in weighing the success of an evangelist, unless one has certain normative, evaluative principles that do not proceed from observation. One can see that a couple stops drinking, or that a couple begins to drink. But a judgment depends, not on this observation, but on whether drinking, or church membership, or anything else, is good or bad. Even church membership may not always be good; and coming forward in an evangelistic campaign may be bad. Mere observation of what happens cannot tell us.

Now, there is one source and only one source from which we may learn how to judge our observations. That source is the Bible.

For one thing, the Scriptures describe several evangelistic endeavors. Unless the methods are definitely condemned, we may infer that these Biblically described methods are permissible, at least under similar conditions. In the second place, and this is more important, the Bible defines what evangelism is. Not every display on the religious page of the Saturday newspaper advertises an evangelistic service that conforms to New Testament standards. Then, in the third place, closely related to point two, the New Testament gives the message that must be preached. And this is the most important point. In the Bible and in the Bible alone can we find what is and what is not Christian evangelism. Several questions have already been asked. Other questions will come on later pages. The answers, all the answers, will be found in Holy Scripture; and if the Scripture does not answer a question, that question has no answer.

Chapter Two
Emotions in the Bible

In view of what has already been said, including the contrast between the formal Lutheran services and all the hot and bother of hillbilly fundamentalism, including therefore the widely held idea that evangelism is at least ninety-nine percent emotion, it will not seem strange to devote some space to a study of emotion. Not only has this question been raised in the previous chapter, not only is its pertinence obvious, but also it will exemplify the method of using the Bible to find answers to the questions we must ask when considering an evangelistic effort for our congregation.

First of all, a short list will be made of happy emotions described in the Bible. In the Psalms there are many instances of God's commanding us to rejoice. Psalm 106:1 says, "Praise ye the Lord." Psalms 146, 147, 148, 149, and 150 open with exactly the same words. No doubt several dozen other verses could be listed. They all show that "Praise is comely for the upright" (Psalm 33:1). There can be no doubt that this applies to evangelistic services as well as to other occasions. There are certain verses in the Bible about mourning, but no one can forbid praise and rejoicing. Philippians 4:4 says, "Rejoice in the Lord alway." I wonder if this applies to an Episcopal funeral? Should we rejoice always? Furthermore, if we were always rejoicing, would rejoicing be an emotion? Emotions are ordinarily thought to be short-lived. An emotional person is one

who changes from day to day, maybe rapidly and unexpectedly.
If a man is always happy, is this an emotion? But before we ask
what an emotion is, let us collect more Scripture passages that
at least seem to be emotional.

In II Samuel 6:12-16 David brought the ark of the Lord
from the house of Obed-edom to Jerusalem with gladness.
David danced before the Lord with all his might. All the house
of Israel shouted, accompanied with the sound of the trumpet.
But Michal, Saul's daughter, David's wife, saw King David
leaping and dancing and despised him in her heart. Well, maybe
the Pentecostalists are right. Shout and dance and make a great
noise! Note in particular that if this was not strictly an
evangelistic service, it was a revival service.

Of course, we must read I Corinthians 14:15 also. Paul
says, "If I pray in an unknown tongue, my spirit prayeth, but my
understanding is unfruitful. What is it then? I will pray with the
spirit, and I will pray with the understanding also; I will sing
with the spirit, and I will sing with the understanding also. Else
. . . how shall . . . the unlearned say 'Amen' . . . seeing he
understandeth not?"

No doubt David understood what he was doing and saying.
It was a very special occasion. The ark had been neglected for
about forty years. Now it was being returned to the Tabernacle.
Maybe this is not a good example to follow in an evangelistic
service. Speaking in tongues also may have been something
unusual and exceptional. During the lifetimes of Christ and the
Apostles God wrought many miracles. Possibly the last previous miracle had been in the time of Daniel. Before that, in the
time of Elijah and Elisha. Miracles occur at times of crisis. They
do not happen every day. They never did. So too with tongues.
These may have been divine signs to accredit the Apostles and
the first preachers of the Gospel. After the establishment of the
Church, these signs ceased. I wonder if the use of the

understanding also was intended to cease with the death of the Apostles? Maybe some other verse will answer this question; but at the moment it is the list of emotions that must be completed.

Not all the emotions in the Bible are so happy. When the Magi rejoiced with exceeding great joy, Herod was wroth; and soon after in Ramah there was a voice heard of lamentation, and weeping, and great mourning. But I guess this does not apply to evangelism.

Back in I Samuel 1:7ff. Hannah wept and did not eat; she was in bitterness of soul and wept sore. Still earlier, obedient Abraham must have been sad when he was told to sacrifice Isaac; and Jacob "refused to be comforted" when his evil sons told him that Joseph had been killed.

There are many examples of sadness and sorrow in the Bible. In Matthew 26:38 Jesus said, "My soul is exceedingly sorrowful, even unto death." If someone should ask, Was Jesus' sorrow an emotion? many people would answer, Yes. But if someone should ask, Was Jesus' sorrow emotional? many people would say, No; and others would be confused. The one person in all the Bible who seems to be the least emotional is Jesus himself. He walks with a calm dignity, and even a detachment, among both friends and enemies. He did not commit himself, even to those who believed on his name, because he knew all men and he knew what was in man. Jesus preached; but he never staged a rip-snorting evangelistic service.

The Beatitudes say, "Blessed are they that mourn." On the day of Pentecost those who heard Peter preach were "pricked in their hearts." It seems that they were agitated about their sins. Peter then told them to repent. Repentance has something to do with a godly sorrow for sin. Should not an evangelist therefore try to produce sorrow and mourning? Should he not try to make his audience uncomfortable? When an evangelist cracks some jokes, and gets the people to sing jingles, jollies them, and makes them laugh, is he doing what the Scripture requires? Is such a service an evangelistic service? Or is it just a floor show that makes light of Christian themes?

I remember an evangelist who came to our church once. He told a joke that depended on a pun made of *veneered* and *very near* Christians. The pun was not particularly good. No one laughed. So he tried to explain his joke: veneer, very near, don't you see? No one laughed. So, I suppose our congregation was catalogued in his mind as a cold, unspiritual group of people. Let the question be put pointedly: Should not an evangelist try to make the people cry instead of laugh? But first, maybe we should ask just what repentance is. Is repentance an emotion? Can one repent without crying? What does it mean to be pricked in the heart? An old Puritan wrote a book, *Alarm to the Unconverted.* Is a fire alarm emotional? If someone cried "Fire!" near you in a crowded building, would you have some emotion? Maybe if you experienced strong emotions, you would lose your head and might fail to escape. Emotion means losing one's head, doesn't it? If not, what is an emotion?

Some examples have now been given of joyous emotions. These are presumably good. Not necessarily, however; for clearly some people rejoice over the wrong things. They may through envy rejoice at the misfortunes of their neighbors. Whether joy and praise are good or evil depends therefore on the intellectual content, *i.e.,* the known object about which one rejoices.

In the second place, examples have been given of sad emotions. These are presumably bad, or at least less than good; but they are understandably appropriate in certain circumstances. Mourning over one's own sins is not only appropriate, but positively good. If not in excess. If not paralyzing and inhibitive of improvement. If not suicidal. Once again, the moral quality of the emotion depends on the object, the situation, the ideas or opinions one has at the time. One cannot say that joy is always good and sadness is always bad. It is like eating fried eggs. In some cases a fried egg sandwich is good, good for you; but not always before going to bed.

Now, in the third place, to continue the list of Biblical emotions, examples must be given of those which most people would deny are good, or even appropriate; but which most people would say are positively evil and bad.

The first is Cain's anger and jealousy that led him to murder Abel. Murder is evil. Let us admit that much. But are anger and jealousy necessarily evil? Consider: "I the Lord thy God am a jealous God, visiting the iniquities of the fathers upon the children unto the third and fourth generation of them that hate me." Consider also: "The Lord, whose name is Jealous, is a jealous God" (Exodus 34:14; compare Deuteronomy 4:24); and Isaiah 42:8, "I am the Lord . . . and my glory will I not give to another." Consider again: "Ye serpents, ye generation of vipers, how can ye escape the damnation of hell?" (Matthew 23:33). Is then anger always evil and is jealousy without exception bad?

Since God has no emotions and is not a man that he should repent, maybe jealousy, wrath, and anger are not emotions. What is an emotion, anyhow? Well, doubtless Cain's anger was emotional, and certainly his murder was a sin.

Is this discussion veering away from the subject of evangelism? No, really it is not. For Cain, after the murder of Abel, had another emotion. It was fear. It might even have been regret. Judas regretted that he had betrayed Christ. Now, if in the evangelist's audience, and all the more in personal individual evangelism, there is a Cain or a Judas—and there often is —the evangelist and the personal worker ought to know something about these emotions. The Bible gives us to believe that neither Cain nor Judas repented. I remember one year when I preached quite a number of sermons in a rescue mission. Nearly always there was a certain man with a red face seated about two-thirds of the way to the back of the room. He always, I think always, cried at the preaching of the Gospel. But I have no reason to think that my evangelistic preaching was successful in the sense of bringing him to Christ. I also remember an example of personal work. In this case the person shed no tears, nor experienced any emotion so far as I could detect. Nor did I make any impassioned appeal. The conversations, over a period of time, would not qualify as "evangelistic" in the hillbilly, stomping, shouting sense. But the observable conduct of the convert over a period of fifteen years now, so far as any man can judge another, testifies to a genuine conversion. This conduct includes faithful attendance at a Bible-believing church, teaching Sunday School classes, attempting to win family and friends, and witnessing in hostile environments. All with as little emotion and as much effectiveness as can be reasonably expected.

With these considerations now in mind, let us add to the list of "bad" emotions a few more Biblical examples.

Probably most people would agree that the emotions of Joseph's brothers just as they were selling him into slavery were bad. They had been thinking about killing him. Instead they sold him for a profit and lied to their father. Clearly emotions are not always good. Sometimes they are sinful. Now, what about David's anger when Nabal would not give food to his men? He and his men had been protecting Nabal's flocks from the attacks of marauding enemies. True, no contract had been signed. But the time of sheep-shearing was a festive occasion and often gifts were distributed. Nabal was a churl, a very nasty man; he would give David nothing; he called him a deserter from his master, Saul. Well, David was angry, very angry. Did he not have a right to be? He determined to kill every man in Nabal's employ. Surely this was going too far. He might have been justified in being angry. He might have been justified in seizing some food. But as for killing the men, he was deterred only by Abigail's intercession.

Laughter can also be a bad emotion, if laughter is an emotion. When Sarah laughed at God's promise of a son in Genesis 18:12, it was bad, of course. Abraham himself also had laughed at God's promise in Genesis 17:17. I am not sure I would have laughed. I might have cried. But neither laughing nor crying could be called good in this situation.

When it is suggested here that some things are good at times and bad at other times, that something is wrong in one case and right in another, do not think that these remarks are a preparation for a defense of situational ethics. Far from it. But there are external actions, and inward thoughts, that are right and good at one time, and evil at another. No one denies that buying a house or going on a picnic is good sometimes and bad other times. So also there is a time to laugh and a time to mourn. This is not situational ethics. The Bible categorically commands, Thou shalt not commit adultery. Adultery is a sin in every situation. There are no exceptions. But the Bible does not command us not to be angry. In fact, the Apostle commands (no doubt for appropriate situations) "Be ye angry, and sin not." But I do not remember any itinerant evangelist telling his audience to be angry. Rather it is, "Everybody happy?" Is this the Biblical method of evangelism? I think not. But the situation is complicated. It is not yet clear what an emotion is. We are not sure whether each item in the Biblical list was an emotion or not. If anyone wants to encourage emotions in evangelism, he ought to know what makes a given state of consciousness an emotion rather than something else. And, equally important, or even more so, it is necessary to know what evangelism is. These questions will now be taken up in order.

Chapter Three

What Is Emotion?

Since the Bible does not define emotion (it does not even use the word), since also one must have some idea of what emotions are, even to make a mere list, not to mention evaluating them, where can one better look than in the writings of modern psychologists? Psychology is held in great repute, especially among the unlearned, and to these people it may come as a surprise that psychologists know very little. But, since no one seems to know any more, and most people know much less, where else shall we look? It is at least worth the try.

In 1962 Robert Plutchik published a small volume entitled *The Emotions.* In its third paragraph he begins to quote from four books, all published since 1925, all of which state that "The confusion and contradiction found today within affective psychology are notorious." Then follow about twenty pages listing a large number of factors that a theory of emotion should unify. The third chapter begins, "The history of psychology is so marked with differences as to the meaning of emotion that some psychologists have suggested that the term be eliminated from psychological writings." One reason the author rejects the James-Lange definition of emotion is that there are emotions no one feels. I would suppose that the majority of evangelists would say that if a person did not feel an emotion, he had no emotion. Obviously, therefore, psychologists are not talking about the same thing evangelists talk about. The word "emotion" means very different things to different people. The author says, "This theory obviously distinguishes between feelings and emotions, a dichotomy characterized by persisting disagreements and ambiguities" (p. 28). Another theory, the motivational theory, so broadens the category of emotion that it includes all psychological processes, with the result that the word "emotion" no longer has any specific significance. The psycho-analytic theory of emotions Dr. Plutchik condemns for "its vagueness and metaphorical character."

The author himself formulates a theory of emotions by following the lead of Descartes, a seventeenth-century philosopher, who classified admiration, love, hate, desire, joy, and sadness as the six primitive "passions;" and all others are combinations of these. Dr. Plutchik also has primitive emotions, or, more accurately, eight prototypic dimensions of emotion: eating, excreting, destroying, protecting, reproducing, depriving, orienting or evaluating, and exploring. These primary emotions are supposed to account for all others. The account can hardly be called satisfactory.*

Like other psychologists, D. O. Hebb (*A Textbook of Psychology*, p. 156) acknowledges that emotion is difficult to define, hard to comprehend, and useless as a scientific term; but in a commonsense way emotion means that something exceptional is going on inside the subject. In this, Hebb no doubt speaks the truth. An emotion is something unusual, sudden, exceptional. If a certain state of consciousness continues over a fairly long period of time, we do not call it an emotion. An emotion is some kind of upheaval within the person. These sudden upheavals evidently occur during evangelistic services.

---

* For other admissions of failure and examples of the unsatisfactory treatment of emotions by psychologists, see *Physiological Psychology*, by Wenger, Jones, and Jones, chapter 21 (Henry Holt and Co., 1956), and *Introduction to Psychology* by Ernest R. Hilgard, chapter 6 (Harcourt, Brace & World, 3rd edition, 1962).

The fact is indisputable. Whether they are helpful or otherwise, whether the evangelist should try to produce them or not try, or even try to prevent them, what their relationship to conversion is—these are questions that are not settled by simply observing that emotions occur.

In addition to the characteristic of suddenly disturbing one's normal mental state, an emotion must be recognized as involuntary. A person does not calmly decide to get angry, or to lapse into depression. Indeed emotions are not only involuntary, in the sense that we do not deliberately choose them, they also occur when we deliberately try to suppress them. At other times we may want to have a certain emotion and yet find that we cannot produce it. Emotion, therefore, is doubly involuntary.

A third characteristic of emotion is the absence of intellectual content. To be sure, we can hardly be angry without being angry at someone or some thing; and this person or thing is known. But the knowledge and the emotion are different, for we can know the person or thing without being angry. The emotion of depression may have no intelligible object at all. Furthermore, the occurrence of the emotion often, perhaps always, makes no change in our knowledge. Emotion therefore has no intellectual content.

Nor should emotion be confused with volition. Among the Protestant Reformers emotion was hardly mentioned at all, while volition was somewhat stressed. In fact the great interest in emotion is rather a modern phenomenon that has so eclipsed the will that this latter now receives scant attention. Thus a most important element of the Christian position has been disparaged. At any rate, we can see that volition is not emotion by the fact that both joy and depression occur without any tendency to act. At most, joy may be accompanied by a tendency to jump, dance, or shout—in some undirected, spontaneous manner—while depression is more a tendency not to act. That a volition or an intellectual act may accompany some emotions cannot be denied; but a dog who accompanies his master on a walk is not for that reason to be identified with the master. If emotion can accompany a volition, then clearly emotion is not volition. Therefore the statement frequently made by modern psychologists, that emotion is (among other things) a tendency to act, is false.

Some further advance may be made, not merely in listing the emotions referred to in the Biblical narrative, but also in evaluating them, by considering the character of God. Does the Bible indicate that God is subject to sudden, involuntary, non-intellectual upheavals in his usually calm state of mind? Well, hardly. The Westminster Confession, the best summary of the contents of the Bible, says that God is without parts or passions. *Parts* refers to bodily organs. Bodies have parts, minds do not. But God is also without passions. The word *passion,* in more modern terminology *affection,* is wider than the term emotion but includes the latter. A passion or affection is the result of being affected by some external force. A dog is affected by a whipping; a student is affected, sometimes, by the possibility of a good grade. There are modern psychology books written about "the affective consciousness." But God is not affected by anything. Or, in another translation of the Greek term, God does not "suffer" anything.

On the contrary, not only the Westminster Confession, but all or nearly all the historic creeds say that God is immutable. He does not change. Emotion, however, is a sudden, involuntary change. To have emotions would be inconsistent with God's eternal state of blessedness.

Now, someone may say that God loves and that love is an emotion. But with respect to love, two points must be made. First, God's love is eternal, therefore not a sudden change, therefore not an emotion. Second, God commands us to love him. A command requires voluntary obedience. Therefore the love God commands is volitional, not emotional. Doubtless God commands the impossible. He commands us to keep his law perfectly. This we cannot do because of sin. The impossibility arises from us; it does not arise from any irrationality in the command. God commands the impossible, but he does not command the absurd. If God commanded us to "emote," it would be the same as commanding a voluntary involuntary act. Here the impossibility resides in the irrationality of the command, not in our physical or moral inability. God cannot command us to draw a plane triangle with just two straight lines —not because of any limitation on his omnipotence, but because the idea of a two-sided triangle is an irrational, self-contradictory idea, and God is not irrational or self-contradictory. But the command, "Emote," is irrational because it would require us to perform voluntarily what is involuntary. Therefore neither God's love nor the human love God commands is emotional: They are volitional. Some other human states of mind, also called love, may of course be emotions, very bad ones.

There is another reason for holding emotions in low esteem. Genesis teaches that man was created in the image of God. Obviously this is something desirable. It distinguishes men from animals. But what is the image of God? Genesis does not make it very plain. However, there are hints in Ephesians and Colossians. These two epistles refer to man's present sinful condition and to his state of innocence before the fall. Regeneration is a kind of recreation, and a restoration, a partial restoration, of innocence. In Ephesians 4:24, after commending Christian maturity in wisdom and knowledge (1:17-18; 4:13-14), Paul says, "Put on the new man that after God hath been created in righteousness and holiness of truth." Here is a reference to creation and the image of God. With the context one may conclude that the image is at least partly a matter of truth, knowledge, righteousness, and holiness. The reference to the image of God is more explicit in Colossians 3:9-10, "Ye have put off the old man with his doings and have put on the new man, that is renewed unto knowledge after the image of him that created him." Here the emphasis falls on knowledge. In all this there is no mention of emotions. Now, the purpose of evangelism is to produce mature Christians, in whom the image of God is renewed. For this purpose knowledge is essential; emotions are not mentioned at all. As was said before, the word emotion does not occur even once in the entire Bible.

It should not be necessary to justify these quotations from the Apostle Paul. One book on evangelism, on its very first page, says Paul never dreamed that people in later ages would be reading his letters. But Paul himself said, "All Scripture is given by the inspiration of God, and is profitable for doctrine." He also said that he received his message by revelation. It is just possible that copies of the Ephesian letter were sent to other churches. And in any case, how could Paul not have expected his letters to be read in all the churches and handed down to their posterity? A book on evangelism that begins by belittling Paul's consciousness of his apostolic authority (and note how Paul defends his authority in Galatians) can hardly be a very good book on evangelism. We judge evangelistic attempts by the Scripture.

In spite of the widespread notion that emotions are desirable, and even essential for conversion, responsible pastors know what trouble emotional people can cause in a church. There was one woman who thought herself very spiritual. She would get wrought up over the least thing and believe it was the working of the Spirit. In some ways she was a good woman. She was very generous. In her own way she was devout. But sometimes she would neglect her housework and her family to spend all night in prayer with some other Pentecostalists downtown. She once burned a closet full of her good clothes because she thought them too good for a Christian. She even thought it sinful to give them to the poor who needed clothes. So she burned them. She was always excitable. She could never talk about any subject, including the Bible, without getting off the track at least twice in every sentence. After changing churches every few months, she stayed with us for two or three years, but finally left because we paid too much attention to the Bible and not enough to the leadings of the Spirit. Going to a church of decidedly different theological complexion, she reported that they believed the same things as we did. A few months later she had changed churches again. This woman did not cause trouble in the sense of disrupting the congregation; she made our work difficult by requiring, or at least needing, a good deal of constant care; and this added burdens and diminished the energy available for other work.

Another case was a man, who, unlike the woman just mentioned, was not mentally unbalanced, but who was also highly excitable. He would imagine that someone in the church slighted him. Then he would air his grievance through the congregation and stir up friction. Ninety-nine percent of the time there was no slight at all. Once he treated one of our elders pretty shabbily, in fact, intolerably. Now, as the elders are supposed to rule the church, and as his conduct had been clearly reprehensible, the elder remonstrated with him somewhat. This threw him into a terrific temper tantrum. The session discussed the whole matter, agreed that the elder in question had been most moderate in the face of provocation, but asked him if he could somehow apologize a little and try to calm things down. The meek and devout elder did so. Finally the man left the church to the relief of the whole congregation.

Very likely emotion is not technically defined as an

unusual, sudden, involuntary, irrational upheaval in one's normal consciousness. This statement may cover emotions and some other mental events besides. For example, a sneeze fits this description, and a sneeze is not an emotion, is it? Well, why couldn't a sneeze be an emotion? We have not satisfactorily defined emotion so as to include all emotions and to exclude all that is not emotion. But perhaps and hopefully our ideas are now a little clearer; we have seen some of the importance of the subject, and with the genus of emotion well enough defined we are prepared to go further into the relationship between emotion and theology.

Chapter Four

Emotion and Theology

The previous chapter should give pause to all those unthinking enthusiasts who take it for granted that emotion is the essential quality of evangelistic meetings. For those who think and do not act so heedlessly there is a more profound and more serious objection to emphasis on emotion. The objection is that reliance on emotion and personal experience is destructive of the Gospel. In fact, reliance on emotion and feeling was the source of modernism. The apostasy of the large denominations today resulted from a deliberate emphasis on feeling and personal experience.

There are some technical complications here. The father of modernism did not so much use the words *emotion* and *feeling.* Whether feeling and emotion are synonyms cannot clearly be decided. It is quite possible that the early modernists did not quite know what they meant by feeling, though it seems that their feelings were less intense than some violent emotions are. One thing, however, is completely clear and indubitable: Feeling is not intellection or cognition. Knowledge is completely excluded. As modernism progressed the feeling on which modernists based their religion was sometimes made analogous to the aesthetic feeling or "aesthetic response." Later it was more neutrally named simply religious experience. How emphasis on feeling or non-cognitive experience produced modernism must now be explained.

Of course, evangelism and Christianity cannot be divorced from experience in one sense of the word. Human life cannot be divorced from experience, for life is experience, if you wish to use the term that way. A child of six experiences learning that two and two are four. All study from first grade through seminary or graduate school is experience. The seminary student experiences the irregular Greek verbs as he memorizes their principal parts. He also experiences bacon and eggs at breakfast. One can avoid experience only by committing suicide; and even then he will have other experiences in the future life. It is personal experience too, vital personal experience, to understand and assent to the doctrine of justification by faith alone, in comparison with which feelings and emotions are trivial. Everything then is experience; but this meaning of the word is so broad that it is useless in discussion. Nor is it what they mean who base religion on experience.

The people who emphasize feelings very stupidly speak as if intellectual experience is not experience. That is to say, they have a narrower view of experience. For them experience is non-intellectual. It is feeling and emotions, while intellectual activity is pictured as superficial and trivial.

Just as it is impossible to conduct or to attend evangelistic services without having experience in the broad sense, so too it is impossible for some people to attend without having emotional experiences. Emotions are involuntary. We may try to suppress them as we try to suppress a sneeze, but often we cannot. The account of Christ's physical sufferings can be so vividly described that few people will be able to remain undisturbed. Whether this is of any spiritual profit is quite another question. People are not ordinarily disturbed when Christ's "descent into hell" is explained as his spiritual separation from his Father. His cry, "I thirst," evoked a little pity even from the throng who watched the crucifixion; but "My

God, my God, why hast thou forsaken me," is not a sure fire ringer in an hysterical camp meeting.

Now, camp meetings, evangelistic extravaganzas, strong insistence on personal experience have largely been recommended as the proper reaction to "dead orthodoxy." There is so little orthodoxy today that I wonder whether perhaps even dead orthodoxy might not be preferred to living heresy. At any rate living heresy in the twentieth century has resulted from reliance on feeling or emotion.

The Pietists of the eighteenth century—an age in which the Lutheran church is said to have been dead—emphasized personal devotion. The intellectual content of Christianity was denounced by philosophers like Kant; the Pietists, though they may not have explicitly denied Christian doctrine, relegated this content to a secondary place. Then since Kant and some others acknowledged some value in a non-intellectual "faith," the Pietistic influence combined with secular philosophy in Friedrich Schleiermacher to produce what we now call modernism.

Schleiermacher, writing in the early nineteenth century, wanted to build religion on such a firm foundation that neither science nor philosophy could attack it. Therefore he based everything on feeling. Whether feeling is the same as emotion hardly makes any difference: Religion, Christianity, were matters of immediate experience. The particular experience he chose was the feeling of absolute dependence. This feeling of dependence gives us the idea of God. That is, he argued, by analyzing the feeling the concept of God is constructed.

Of course, according to Schleiermacher, we have no knowledge of *God*. At most we know, or better, feel his *relation* to us; and this relation is this feeling. Other doctrines, supposedly Christian doctrines, can likewise be obtained by analyzing experience. By rather specious analyses Schleiermacher thought he was able to deduce the doctrine of the Trinity, the Atonement, and even the Lord's Supper. Theology is really psychology.

There are three points that especially need to be noted in this attempt to base Christianity on experience. The first is that the derivation of the doctrines is suspect. It is worse than suspect. It is ludicrous. There is just no possible logical way of analyzing an emotion or a feeling and proving the doctrine of the Trinity. The doctrine of the Trinity is found only in the Biblical revelation. No one would ever have thought of it, no one ever did think of it, apart from the Bible. True, some philosophers had three-fold sets of principles. Plato had the world of Ideas, the Demiurge, and chaotic Space. But this is not a tri-personal divine being. Plotinus had something similar. He spoke of the One, the Ideas, and the Soul. But he also had a Logos and a lower world. The whole was continuous. There is no tri-personal supreme being. Plotinus's One does not think and cannot know. Neo-Platonism is not at all similar to trinitarian Christiani⁺v. Schleiermacher therefore did not get the Trinity from Christian experience. One may doubt that his experience was Christian, anyway.

But there is also a second point to notice. Schleiermacher expressed a basic desire to make Christianity immune from scientific objections. Miracles are impossible. Therefore one must reject much of the Bible, if he wishes to make Christianity palatable to the modern mind. This is permissible because the Bible couches its beneficial message in the limited thought forms of a by-gone age. The precious kernel is wrapped around with worthless husks. Discard the husks and preserve the essential ideas.

But what is essential? Shortly after the death of Schleiermacher and under the influence of Hegel, the modernists concluded that the personality of God was not essential to

Christianity. In fact, Schleiermacher himself was a pantheist. In philosophical writings it is quite clear that he had no sympathy for the theory of a personal God. But in his religious writings he tried to accommodate himself to the prejudice of common Christian opinion. His language therefore at times sounds semi-orthodox. But by 1850 there was quite a volume of theological writing that denied the personality of God.

Naturally also the atonement was considered unessential. After all, experience does not justify such a doctrine. It is repulsive to man's moral sensibilities. It conflicts with moral experience. And of all things, the moral principles of the Sermon on the Mount are the essential kernel of Christianity. As Renan and others who wrote on the historical Jesus said, the real Jesus who stands behind the legends of the Gospels was a mild ethical teacher who had no theology at all.

There is a third point. It is one on which Hegel indulged in some ridicule. The point has to do with the particular emotion, the feeling of dependence, that Schleiermacher thought to be the key to religion. Said Hegel, "If feelings are to constitute the basic condition of the essence of man, then he would be on the same level as animals, for it is inherent in animals to have their condition in and to live according to feelings. If religion in a human being is founded only on feeling, the latter has no other function than to be the feeling of his dependency, and thus a dog would be the best Christian, for it possesses this feeling most intensely and lives mainly in it. A dog even has feelings of 'salvation' when its hunger is satisfied by a bone."

There is a serious implication in this jibe. Later modernistic theologians rejected the feeling of dependence in favor of something more appropriate. One suggested the "sense of the holy." Others posited a religious experience *sui generis*, just as the aesthetic experience is *sui generis*. Still others widened the meaning of religious experience to take in all feelings of value.

They also rejected Schleiermacher's (quasi) Protestant inter-pretation and aimed to find a universal religion. Two results followed. On this empirical ground religion excludes all knowledge of God. Even Schleiermacher understood this. At best the analysis of experience gives us only so much knowl-edge of our feelings. There is not the remotest possibility of arriving at the doctrine of justification or anything else specifically Christian. The second result is that with the exclusion of Christian themes, modernism developed into humanism and atheism. Or, at most, the "god" of the humanists is no better than the "no-god" of the atheists, and is definitely worse than the "all-god" of the pantheists.

The result of excluding from religion everything except what could be analyzed out of experience can be seen, in one case, in the work of Professor H.N. Wieman. He defined God as "that character of events to which man must adjust himself in order to attain the greatest goods and avoid the greatest ills." God is not a person. God is not transcendent. He is not even the whole world, as in pantheism. For Wieman God is not even a series of events. He, or, better, it is simply some characteristics of events; for this is the only sort of god that can be deduced from or made conformable to experience.

By the time of Wieman in the twentieth century, or very soon after him, even the morality of the Sermon on the Mount goes the way of the Atonement and the Resurrection. Now we have situation ethics; and Joseph Fletcher asserts that every one of the Ten Commandments should be broken. Experiences, the situations in which we find ourselves, determine what we should do. And if in a particular situation we see value in committing adultery, by all means commit adultery. Fletcher's wording is about as near to commending suburban clubs for wife swapping as language can come without being absolutely explicit.

Some of our anti-theological, pietistic friends will hold up their hands in horror and exclaim that such things do not agree with their experience. In this, however, they are mistaken for two reasons. First, even if it were true that their experience somehow condemns situational ethics, who are they to exalt their experience above the experience of others? If religion is to be based on experience, it is to be based on the experience of each person. One person's experience is as normative as another's. No doubt some people do not find wife swapping valuable. But some do. The appeal is to experience. But my experience is not a norm for you, or vice versa. I like oysters, you may not. The Spanish Catholics like to torture bulls in their bull fights. The Puritans do not like this. But I cannot force you to like oysters; nor do you have any right to deny them to me. Hence my religion is based on my experience and you can base yours on yours.

If religion is not to be thus entirely individual and personal, but if it is to preserve some universality, then one must deduce this universal religion only from those experiences which all men find valuable. Individual objections to bull fights and adultery do not count. All that counts is that on which all men agree. But this is very little. And advanced humanism, as exemplified in Edwin A. Burtt, restricts religious prescriptions to the search for health, wealth, beauty, truth, and friendship. But such prescriptions are useless in determining which course of action one should take in a given situation. Should I attend church? Should I take my vacation in Arizona or Florida? Should I love my neighbor's wife? Humanism has no answer to such specific questions. No universal answer, that is; there can be no universal prescription against theft or profanity. Each person does as he pleases. And as humanism cannot rule this life, so also it has no hope of heaven in the next.

The Pietists, and all others who think Christianity is based on experience, are mistaken. It is not true that their experience condemns situational ethics. Of course each Pietist condemns this. But there is nothing in his experience that logically compels him to do so. My distaste for oysters does not justify laws condemning oysters and sauerkraut. If beyond this we try to justify any line of conduct, or condemn any, by an appeal to the common characteristics of all human experience, the result will be equally negative. There may be no universal characteristic at all. And if there is, it would be something like pain and pleasure, which are so general that no particular conclusion can come from them. Universal experience does not commend even truth and beauty. One could not even conclude that one ought to avoid pain and seek pleasure. The fact that all men dislike pain does not prove that it should be avoided. Maybe it is a means to a more valuable end. Whether it is or not cannot be determined by analyzing pain and pleasure. Experience teaches us nothing!

The Bible does. If we base our religion on divine revelation instead of experience, we will have the Trinity, the Atonement, the Resurrection, a great deal of intellectual theology, and the morality of the Sermon on the Mount as well. But unless God tells us these things, we could not know them. Buddhism may be based on experience, on someone's experience; but Christianity is based on the Bible, on divine revelation, not on emotion.

Chapter Five

What Is Evangelism?

If the heedless evangelist gives no thought to the place or desirability of emotion and experience in his services, if now it is clear that he should, then all the more should he stop a moment to ask what evangelism is. At first he might simply snort at such a question. Doesn't he know good and well what evangelism is? Isn't he a professional evangelist? Evangelism then is what he does, and his doing it makes it evangelism.

If, on the other hand, the activity is to be Christian and not mere entertainment, one might acknowledge that Christ and the Apostles had some idea of evangelism, and just perhaps our practices should be judged by theirs. Even the usage of the word in the New Testament should be informative.

To evangelize is to preach the Gospel. The Gospel is the evangel. In Greek the word is *evangelion*. The verb too, translated *preach* or *proclaim*, has the same root. It is *evangelid-zomai*. The noun occurs about 75 times in the New Testament: four times in Matthew, and five times in Mark. The opening words of the second Gospel are, "The beginning of the Gospel . . ." and the account, the Gospel itself, follows. The Gospel is what Mark wrote down; or at least what Mark wrote down is the beginning of the Gospel.

Mark 1:15 commands us to "believe in the Gospel."* Some people make a distinction between believing a written account and believing in a person. This verse undermines such a distinction. Really, when one believes *in* a person, he believes the words the person speaks—he believes his promises and his asserted ability to perform. This is what is meant by saying that we trust a person.

The other references in Mark (8:35, 10:29, 13:10, 14:9, and 16:15) all indicate that the Gospel is a message that must be published, proclaimed, or preached. That the Gospel is a message is emphasized in Acts 15:7. "Peter rose up" in the Jerusalem Council, "and said . . . God made choice among us that the Gentiles by my mouth should hear the word of the Gospel and believe." The *words* came from Peter's *mouth*, and these words are what these Gentiles believed.

In addition to Romans 1:9 and 10:16, chapter 2:16 says that "God shall judge . . . according to my Gospel." Paul had been preaching certain standards of justice; he had been condemning sin; he was in the process of exposing the wickedness of the Jews. In this verse he says that God's judgment will be based on the principles of justice that he has been expounding. To be sure, chapter two does not expound all the Gospel; but the Gospel contains these principles by which God judges. If we today are to preach the Gospel, rather than some other message, the ideas of this chapter, Romans 2, must be included. Some recent books on evangelism say they should not.

It would be tedious to quote all 75 verses that use the word *Gospel;* but I Corinthians 15:1 contains a part of the message

---

* In Greek the object of the verb *believe* can be a simple noun in the dative case, or a noun preceded by the prepositions *en, eis,* or *epi,* and sometimes *peri.* There seems to be no obvious distinction in meaning among these forms. In Hebrew also two prepositions are possible.

not mentioned in Romans 2. In brief it says, "The Gospel which I preached unto you [explains] . . . how that Christ died for our sins . . . and that he rose again the third day . . . ." This is the Gospel "by which also ye are saved." The Gospel therefore is a message, not an emotion. And as a message it is received by the intellect, not the emotions. In Philippians 1:27 Paul tells us to let our conversation or conduct accord with the Gospel, which we can do by being of one mind, striving together for the faith of the Gospel. Note that Paul tells us to be of one mind. He does not tell us to be of one emotion. Now, since as Colossians 1:5 says, the Gospel is the word of truth, its reception has to be an intellectual act. Truth cannot be received by the emotions. A message is something intelligible. It is something to be understood. If the facts of Christ's death and resurrection were not to be understood, then music and painting could replace preaching and words; for the arts can stimulate emotion, but they cannot convey the Gospel. See also Colossians 1:23.

The verb *evangelize* occurs over fifty times in the New Testament. It is most often translated *preach.* There is no point in multiplying quotations. The Gospel is clearly a message to be proclaimed, understood, and in order for a person to be saved, believed. John Brown of Edinburgh in *An Exposition of the Epistle of Paul to the Galatians* (p. 170), chapter three, verse twenty-three, said, "But before faith came. . . . Some interpreters understand by 'faith' Jesus Christ, whom they represent as the object of faith. . . . In a strict propriety of language it is not Jesus Christ personally considered, but the truth about Jesus Christ, which is the object of faith. . . ."

The point is particularly appropriate for the present days of apostasy. The liberals use the name Jesus Christ, and some other historic terms, as symbols to evoke pious emotions. The phrases often sound good. But after a little study we discover that their Jesus was not born of a virgin, never raised Lazarus from the dead, and never himself came out of the tomb. Their Jesus is an empty name without intellectual content, a mere emotional idol. Real Christians believe the truth about Jesus: that he actually was virgin-born, that he actually said, "The Son of Man came . . . to give his life a ransom for many," and that this is precisely what he did on the cross. It is the intellectual content, the message, that counts.

There is more to be said about the Gospel message. In particular an explanation is needed of the way an evangelist's evaluation of emotion causes him to alter the message, either by the inclusion of certain topics or by the exclusion of others. However, before showing how an evangelist selects his message, the aim of the evangelist should be considered.

The unthinking evangelist has a ready made answer with respect to his aim. Obviously his aim is to win souls. Why does this need thought? Is it not obvious? No, it is not quite obvious. In fact, this simple, unthinking answer is too simple and too unthinking. If this is the limit of the evangelist's aim, his conduct of the evangelistic campaign will most likely be somewhat unscriptural.

That there be no misunderstanding, let it be made quite clear that this answer is not exactly wrong. Of course the preaching of the Gospel aims at the salvation of souls. It was said at the outset that the Church must gather in those that are being saved, unless it is to die in this generation. And the zeal of some thoughtless evangelists is highly commendable in itself, even if it is not according to knowledge. It would be most gratifying if all who had knowledge had the same degree of zeal as some of our enthusiastic brethren. Nevertheless the answer is too simple.

It is too simple because it is too short, too ambiguous, and too easily misunderstood. Yet, if properly defined, it is entirely scriptural. Jude in verse 23 says, "Others [you are to] save, snatching them out of the fire." James 5:20 says, "He that converteth a sinner . . . shall save a soul from death." I Timothy 4:16 reads, "Take heed, for in doing this thou shalt both save thyself and them that hear thee." In I Corinthians 9:22 the Apostle claims that "I am made all things to all men that I might save some." Compare Romans 11:14. Peter in Acts 2:40 tells his audience, "Save yourselves."

But is it true that a man can save himself? Did Paul save anybody? Can one man convert another? What about grace? Is not salvation of the Lord? James, who in the verse quoted said that one man should convert another, also says "There is one lawgiver who is able to save and destroy." And he also says, "The engrafted word . . . is able to save your souls." The angel told Joseph to call his name Jesus, "for he shall save his people from their sins." And the children of Israel, in times of repentance, called on the Lord to save them. Then of course there is that very familiar verse, "By grace are ye saved, through faith, and that not of yourselves, it is the gift of God."

In salvation, or more particularly, in regeneration, in the production of faith, how much is to be attributed to the evangelist? How much is to be attributed to the sinner? How much is to be attributed to God? There are not many, I suppose that there are not any American fundamentalist evangelists who accept the views of Pelagius. This monk of the fifth century took the idea of saving yourself very seriously. Each man really saved himself. The messenger could repeat to him the commandments of God, and God had been gracious in giving the law, but all else was to be accomplished by the person himself. He was able to keep God's commandments; sin had no great hold on him; and by becoming law-abiding, he would save himself. But I have never heard any evangelist talk like this. There are, however, some people I would not call evangelists who talk very much like this. These are the liberals who want us to get "involved" in all sorts of street demonstrations, who want us to engineer boycotts of firms that manufacture munitions for our nation, who want us to disrupt the orderly procedures of democratic government, and thus we shall save ourselves— from what and to what I cannot tell.

Nearly all the popular evangelists split up the credit a bit more equitably. Some credit goes to the evangelist, some to the person converted, and of course a fair percentage to God. The evangelist preaches the message, and as James said, the word preached saves the man. (Is this just what James said?) Then of course, God and only God can regenerate. But God regenerates only those who by their own will have manufactured their faith in Jesus Christ. Faith is not a gift; it is something we ourselves do. And until we do it, God will not help.

Then there are other preachers; they are not what anybody would call popular evangelists; and these men say something immensely different. To be sure, they grant that the evangelist does something. The aim of evangelism, that is, the aim of preaching the Gospel, is to present to the sinner the message to be believed. Faith cometh by hearing, and hearing by the word of God. The Christian witness certainly has a part in the process of salvation. But it is not the decisive part. Then the sinner has a part too. He must listen to the message. We can say more. He must understand the message. If a missionary went to the Chinese or the Zambians and preached in English, they could not understand him, and they would not believe the Gospel because they would not have heard the message. Understanding is essential. But it is not decisive, for many people hear the message and understand it very well, but they do not believe it. For example, Saul as a young man heard the message. He understood it better than most of the Christians did. It was because he understood it so well that he became a persecutor. Jesus is God; he said to himself: This is blasphemy; these people must be exterminated. So he harried them, beat them, and imprisoned them. He understood the Gospel, but he did not believe it. Note also that when he believed, it was the same Gospel he had earlier heard. Later on, when he had retired to Arabia for meditation and for revelation, he learned more. God told him additional truths. These he learned directly from God, for he did not confer with those who were apostles before him. He conferred with God. But at the moment of conversion, he understood no more than he had already heard.

This brings the discussion to the matter of faith or belief. Now, who does this? To whom is the credit? Not the evangelist of course, unless you wish to credit him with extreme powers of persuasion. It is to the credit either of the sinner or of God. One thing is clear. It is the sinner who believes. God is not the believer. It is we who must have faith. If God can be said to have faith in any sense, it is entirely irrelevant to the problem of evangelism. The sinner has the faith. No one else.

But is the credit his? The familiar verse quoted before is "For by grace are ye saved through faith; and that not of yourselves: it is the gift of God."* Here the apostle tells us by revelation that faith is the gift of God. The credit then belongs to God. A man in the exercise of his natural powers given him by creation may understand the Gospel; but no sinner by the exercise of his natural powers believes that Jesus is Lord. This belief is the gift of God. Of course, it is the sinner who believes; no one else can believe for him, not even God. Believing is a mental act, and it is individual and personal. But it is God and God alone who causes a man to believe. The man simply does

---

* Those who say that the word *faith* in Greek is feminine and the word *that* is neuter, and that therefore the demonstrative pronoun cannot refer to faith, know very little Greek. Many evangelists know very little Greek. They should learn that feminine abstract nouns frequently take neuter pronouns, and that even feminine concrete nouns sometimes take neuter pronouns.

the act because God made him do it. It is to God's credit—or in more scriptural language, it is to the praise of the glory of his grace, and of his mere good pleasure.

There is more to it than this. God has a method by which he causes a sinner to believe. Saul was a sinner, unregenerate, dead in trespasses and sins. So at one time were the Ephesians. So were we. But God who is rich in mercy, even when we were dead in sins, has raised us from the dead with Christ, for by grace are ye saved, not of works, lest any man should boast. Evangelist John calls this action of God regeneration. He says that those who believe have been born, not of the will of the flesh, but they have been born of God. The other three evangelists usually refer to this as God's giving us life. Now, faith is the exercise of the powers of spiritual life. A dead man cannot exercise the functions of life. A spiritually dead man cannot believe. As Jesus said to the Pharisees, "How can ye believe?" The dead cannot believe. Therefore God must give the dead sinner life, and the first function of that new life is to believe the Gospel. The glory therefore is God's.

This is why there is a third aim for the evangelist. And this third aim is the most important and most profound. The ultimate aim is not to convert sinners. Nor is it to preach the Gospel. It is to glorify God. After speaking about the unsearchable riches of Christ, Paul says that God created the universe in order that his manifold wisdom should be revealed (by means of the Church which is built up by evangelism) to the principalities and powers in the heavenly realm. The glory then belongs to God, in or by means of the Church and Jesus Christ, to all generations of the age of ages. Amen.

To glorify God it is necessary to preach the Gospel. If the aim were to save souls, maybe some persuasive hocus pocus could produce results as spectacular as those seen in mammoth meetings. But it is God with whom we have to do, God, before whose eyes all things are open and manifest. Hocus pocus may impress men, but it cannot fool God. To glorify God, his message must be preached. Alterations, dilutions, additions, falsifications are prohibited. Now, just what this message is, what parts of it should be preached, what parts should not be preached, and whether musical saws and klaxon horns should be used—all these things are decided upon by the evangelist largely on the ground of his notion of the role of emotion in evangelism. How this is so can be seen by a study of a small booklet entitled *Fundamentalism and Evangelism,* by John R.W. Stott. I wish to show how he distorts the Biblical Gospel because of his views on the aim of evangelism and his evaluation of emotion and intellect.

In chapter one Mr. Stott makes some admirable statements about the Bible. He notes that if Christ was sinless, he must have told the truth. He was inerrant (p. 17). Although he seems to avoid the words *inerrant* and *infallible* with respect to the apostles, Mr. Stott remarks on their claim to divine authority. "They teach with dogmatic emphasis." And "Paul boldly links together God's teaching and his own apostolic charge." In addition there are several other excellent statements on the nature of Scripture. All this should be taken as Mr. Stott's acceptance of the doctrine of verbal and plenary inspiration and his adherence to the complete truth, the inerrancy and infallibility of Scripture in its entirety.

Unfortunately, in the United States at least, some so-called Evangelicals are claiming to accept the "authority" of Scripture, even while asserting that it contains errors. I know one queer duck who says he believes in infallibility but not in inerrancy. Or is it the other way around? Liberals are often dishonest. Since by and large they commit perjury when they take their ordination vows—accepting the Westminster Confession in the vow, but not believing many of the doctrines it enumerates—it is not wise to trust their use of words. The best words I know for the present situation are: verbal and plenary inspiration, and inerrant and infallible.

Now, I am far from accusing Mr. Stott of dishonesty. Fifty years ago his words would have been taken as synonymous with or equivalent to the Reformation doctrine of verbal and plenary inspiration. The trouble is that liberal laxness with language, and the deliberate attempt to confuse people in order to gain political power in the churches, makes it difficult to know what an honest man wants to say.

If Mr. Stott did not accept the Bible as the inerrant word of God, I would not take the trouble, in a book on evangelism, to object to his view of the emotions and the content of the Gospel. These are matters that can be discussed only on the basis of Scripture. If one of us believes the Bible and the other does not, no progress could be made in discussion. One might show that the Bible teaches this or that, while the other could reply, Of course it does, but I do not accept it. This latter person uses an external criterion to judge what parts of the Bible are true and what parts are false. His external criterion is probably some form of empirical philosophy. But the Bible-believer cannot base his arguments on such a platform, but on revelation only. Assuming now that Mr. Stott does in fact believe the Bible, one can profitably discuss with him whether the Scripture teaches such and such, and whether one of us is introducing something foreign and secular into our view of the Scriptural message. This is the nature of my criticism. I wish to show that his view of emotion, of mind, of the Biblical word *heart* is not Scriptural and that because of mistaken views on these terms, he alters the contents of the Gospel.

Chapter two of his booklet (it has only two chapters for a total of forty-one pages) is headed *Evangelism*, and it begins with an account of the mind or understanding. After a very few admissions that man is not like a mule that has no understanding and that we should love the Lord with all our mind, Mr. Stott puts some pages of emphasis on the fact that the mind of man is sinful. One of his conclusions is that "we will need to be cautious in relying too greatly on the mind when making an evangelistic appeal."

He immediately makes some concessions. The evangelist will seek to give a reasoned and reasonable exposition of God's plan of salvation. We must remember that "the New Testament represents conversion in terms of our response not to a Person but to the truth." He also notes that the Apostles "reason and argue" with their hearers. These concessions are admirable. But why should not these Scriptural themes have received the *emphasis;* why should not the *concession* have been simply to be a little cautious?

In these days particularly, so it seems to me, a strong emphasis on the intellect is necessary. The temper of the times is nihilistic. The authors are irrationalistic. Nothing is true. One must act on hunches. One must decide blindly. Logic is deceptive. Argument is decadent. Thus we have dialectical theologians, existentialists, hippies, and violent street demonstrations. In view of all this, it is good to repeat what the Scripture says. It says a great deal. One could go through I John, the Proverbs, passages in I Corinthians, and many individual verses; but here for an example two chapters of Ephesians will be used.

In Ephesians 1:8 Paul tells us that God has abounded to us in all wisdom and prudence. He does not mean that God acted wisely and prudently. He means that God makes us act wisely and prudently. He does this by making known to us the secret of his will. In verse 13 we hear the word of truth. In the seventeenth verse Paul prays that God grant us a spirit of wisdom in knowing him; which comes about by the eyes of our heart being enlightened. In a moment or two it will be shown that *heart* is a Scriptural expression for mind. It does not means emotions. Here the heart is enlightened so that knowledge results. And Paul continues to pray that we should know a great deal (verse eighteen).

The second chapter of Ephesians does not use the word *knowledge,* but it is full of knowledge that we should learn. Then in chapter three the emphasis on knowledge resumes. God made known something to Paul, and as we read him we can understand his understanding about the secret that God has now more fully revealed. In verse eight Paul brings to light, *i.e.* makes known, the administration of God's plan—God who created the world so that principalities and powers should know the wisdom of God. In 3:18 Paul prays that we may grasp or understand the breadth and length of God's love; and then he makes a very paradoxical statement. This love exceeds knowledge but we are to have knowledge of this love that exceeds knowledge. He almost says we should know the unknowable. What is more, we are to know what exceeds knowledge in order to be filled to all the fulness of God. The whole is an amazing paragraph. Its emphasis on knowledge is most important today.

Contrasted with this passage of Scripture, Mr. Stott's denigration of the mind is all the more distressing, for when he comes to speak of emotion, he does not say that the emotions are sinful. Everything he says in sub-section (ii) is in commendation of the emotions.

This perverse evaluation is certainly not Scriptural. Mr. Stott tries to make it seem so by saying, "Jesus told us to love the Lord our God with all our *heart* as well as with all our mind." But Mr. Stott seems to have little idea of what the *heart* means in Scripture. His context shows that he thinks the Bible is talking about the emotions when it uses the word *heart.* But if anyone would take a few moments and look up every instance of this word in the Old Testament, he would find that about seventy-five percent of the time, it means the mind. The remaining one fourth of the instances are divided between the will and the emotions. Strictly the word *heart,* it seems to me, means "the whole personality." And the proportion shows that the mind is the most important factor in the whole personality. At any rate, the word is not the equivalent of the emotions.

Now, before going on and showing how this unscriptural view causes Mr. Stott to alter the contents of the Gospel, I think it essential to stress the fact that man is sinful. And if man is sinful, so is his mind. So are his emotions.

The Scripture pictures an unregenerate farmer doing his spring ploughing, and it says that even the ploughing of the wicked is sin. No matter what an unregenerate man does, it is a sin. This Biblical theme is well summarized by the Westminster Confession in chapter 16, paragraph 7: "Works done by unregenerate men, although, for the matter of them, they may be things which God commands . . . yet, because they proceed not from a heart purified by faith . . . they are therefore sinful. . . . And yet their neglect of them is more sinful and displeasing to God."

Let strong emphasis therefore be placed on the sinfulness of man. Man is dead in sins and is totally unable to do any spiritual good. For this reason an evangelist may well be cautious in relying too greatly on the mind. He should be cautious in relying too greatly on the man. The evangelist should rely wholly on the Holy Ghost to regenerate his auditors.

But though we should not rely "too greatly" on the mind for something it cannot at all do, still the mind, sinful though it is, can exercise its natural functions. Mr. Stott says (page 23), "the human mind is both finite and fallen, and will neither understand nor believe without the gracious work of the Holy Spirit." Most emphatically, the unregenerate man cannot believe or have faith without the irresistible work of the Holy Spirit. But he can understand the Gospel with the mind as it is. If he could not understand the message, why preach it? Why in particular should a missionary spend years in hard labor learning a foreign language, if his hearers cannot understand the message? Why should he not preach to them in English? In the providence of God, faith, though it be the gift of God, is given through hearing. And it is not through hearing an unknown tongue, but through understanding an intelligible message.

With this distortion of the Scriptural position, it is not surprising that Mr. Stott fails to insist on the preaching of the Gospel as the Gospel is found in the Bible. There are probably other factors besides his view of the emotions that contribute to this result. He seems to be influenced by some phases of the current dialectical theology. Yet this influence is not very far removed from the matter of emotions, for the dialectical theologians do not hold the intellect in esteem as did the Reformers. Some of them explicitly repudiate logic and intelligibility. If they do not explicitly arouse the emotions, they may nonetheless be thought of as mystics.

In contradiction to the Bible and to Paul's example, Mr. Stott says that "Our objective is not to unfold to him [the unsaved person] 'the whole counsel of God' but to proclaim the essential core of the Christian gospel." In this connection, note very carefully that Paul claimed that he was innocent of the blood of all men because he had declared all the counsel of God. There is no hint that an evangelist should be silent and omit certain sections of God's revelation. Admittedly a preacher must begin at the point where his hearers find themselves. When Peter preached to the Jews, he did not have to repeat all the Old Testament. Much of it he could take for granted. But when Paul preached on Mars Hill, he could not assume that the Athenians had a knowledge of the Old Testament, or even of its basic theism. So that was where he began. But there is no hint that that is where he wanted to end. His hearers walked out on him; but had they stayed, he would have continued.

Mr. Stott says, "It is commonly accepted today that within the New Testament itself a distinction is made between the kerugma (the proclamation of the gospel) and the didaché (the instruction of converts)." True, this idea is commonly accepted today. It is one of the most important parts of the anti-scriptural theories of the dialectical theolgians. And it should be resisted by those who believe the Bible.

For one thing, the idea of finding a kernel, or a few important themes, and discarding the rest as unessential, raises the question as to how one should distinguish what is important from what is unimportant. In the history of modernism from Schleiermacher to contemporary times, this kernel has contracted to zero. Modern modernism no longer has even God. God is dead. The kernel is an existential experience or a march on a picket line or the disrupting of democratic procedures in favor of mob violence.

No doubt Mr. Stott would object most strongly to such irresponsible actions; but when a person begins to pare off parts of the Gospel as unessential, there is no stopping point.

That the paring off and omissions have no stopping point can be seen by reflecting on another of Mr. Stott's statements. He says, "The evangelist cannot be expected to usurp the task of the pastor or the teacher. Nor can he, especially in an inter-denominational mission, trespass into disputed and controversial fields."

These two sentences are full of misunderstanding and confusion. Note that the word *usurp* is a loaded word. Its use is to picture the evangelist as doing something that it is not his business to do. But if the evangelist's duty is to preach the Gospel, he must preach what the pastor preaches, and he does so without usurpation. An itinerant evangelist should be looked upon as a person who in some way can make a more forceful appeal than the pastor. The pastor is without honor in his own pulpit. The stranger is a bit exceptional. He attracts a little extra attention. But the message must be the same, the same Biblical message, without turning aside to the right or the left, without addition or subtraction.

In the next place, Mr. Stott's second sentence is impossible of attainment. I have never known an evangelist to avoid all controversial topics. Dr. Billy Graham, when in Indianapolis, spent ten minutes attacking Presbyterian doctrine. He told his audience that it was useless to pray for the people who had come forward in response to his invitation. Not even God could help them. They could rely only on their own will. He also said many other controversial things. So too did this evangelist whose preaching I described on the first page of *Biblical Predestination,* from whose use of words I chose the title of that work. In fact, I must say that I strongly detest the hypocrisy of evangelists who object to others preaching on controversial themes and themselves do the same. Does it not occur to them that if our preaching is controversial because it conflicts with theirs, theirs is just as controversial because it conflicts with ours? They make such an accusation against us so as to deflect attention from their own methods. Now, I do not condemn controversy. The whole of the Bible is controversial. What I detest is hypocrisy.

Now, for all of Mr. Stott's complaint against controversial topics, he himself is engaging in controversy by recommending his type of evangelism. It is controversial to pare off parts of the Gospel. Any paring is controversial. Even after he has pared, controversy remains. It is clear that Mr. Stott stops paring before the Atonement is discarded. But the Atonement is a very controversial doctrine. And I wish to controvert what Mr. Stott says about the Atonement.

The Bible teaches that Christ's death was a propitiatory sacrifice. The modernist Revised Standard Version mistranslates the Greek text in an effort to omit propitiation. Now, Mr. Stott says, "We emphatically do not believe that He did this to placate and buy off the anger of God." On the contrary, we emphatically do believe it. Only it is not the same "we." Mr. Stott is engaging in interdenominational controversy. Some groups do not believe that Christ gave his life as a ransom, a payment to the Father, to buy off sinners from the Father's wrath. Some do so believe. So do the Scriptures. Romans 1:18 is a verse that speaks of God's wrath and anger. Christ's denunciations of the Pharisees stress the wrath of God. Hell is the punishment inflicted on the unsaved, and is referred to as the wrath to come. Christ interposed himself in a propitiatory sacrifice to save his own from this wrath. He is called the Lamb of God, and the whole Mosaic sacrificial system anticipates this final sacrifice. Even the covenant with Noah, which the dispensationalists try to reduce to politics, and in which they see no reference to the Atonement, speaks of placating an angry God. This idea is obscured in the King James version, and the American version as well. These translations say that God smelled a sweet odor. But the Koehler-Baumgartner lexicon (the latest lexicon at this writing) gives just one meaning to the Hebrew word transliterated *niychoach: appeasement (Beschwichtigung)*. The "smell of appeasement" then means the placating odor. See also the verbal usage in Ezekiel 5:13, "I will appease my anger." Hence the correct translation of Genesis 8:20-21 is, "And Noah builded an altar unto the Lord . . . and offered burnt offerings on the altar. And the Lord smelled the placating odor."

Thus anticipations of Christ's sacrifice in the Old Testament and explanations of his sacrifice in the New agree that he was the propitiation for our sins. He turned aside God's wrath and anger, which we deserved.

To deny this, as Mr. Stott does, is at the very least to initiate a controversy at the very center of the Gospel. In my opinion, it is something much worse: It is a rejection of the Gospel. Do away with Christ's propitiation and his satisfaction of the Father's justice, and you do away with Christianity. I pray that Mr. Stott does not mean what his words say.

But his words are clear, and they must be rejected if one is to be true to the Bible. Speaking of the "fact" of the cross, Mr. Stott says (page 35), "Our desire is that men should believe that fact, not accept our explanations. 'Christ died for our sins' is enough without any further elucidation. Moreover, our appeal is never that men should accept a theory about the Cross but that they should receive a Person who died for them."

These statements are one hundred percent wrong. They should be denied with all vehemence. They are completely anti-scriptural and totally destructive of Biblical Christianity.

In the first place, Mr. Stott's antithesis here between receiving a Person and believing a theory is inconsistent with the Scripture references he himself previously quoted to the effect that the New Testament represents conversion in terms of our response not to a Person but to the truth. In addition, John Brown of Edinburgh was quoted on this point just a page or two ago. For further emphasis note also this passage from Klaas Runia, in his *Reformation Today* (p. 56): "One of the most popular slogans in contemporary theology is that truth in the New Testament does not mean doctrinal truth about Christ but a personal knowledge of Christ. We believe that such a contrast between propositional conceptual truth (truth about) and personal truth (knowledge 'of') is utterly foreign to the New Testament."

In the second place, Mr. Stott's antithesis between a fact and a theory contradicts the whole New Testament. The "fact" of the Cross is that the Romans executed a man by nailing him to a post. It is also a fact that there were two other men crucified that day. From the standpoint of "fact" all three fit the description. But if there is any difference between the significance of Christ's death and the death of the thieves, it is a matter of "explanation" and not of "fact." Death may be a fact; but propitiation is an explanation or theory. And it is the theory that counts.

In the third place, when Mr. Stott says, " 'Christ died for our sins' is enough without any further eludication," he contradicts his previous words and contradicts Scripture as well. He contradicts his previous words because the phrase "for our sins" itself goes beyond "fact" and is a theory. He contradicts Scripture because I Corinthians says, "Christ died for our sins *according to the Scriptures.*" The Scriptures give a great deal of further elucidation. The theory that "Christ died for our sins . . . without . . . further elucidation" is a poor theory and an anti-scriptural one.

Some people think that Christ died for our sins as an example to us of courage or martyrdom. His death exerts a moral influence on us. In this sense Christ died for our sins. But preaching the death of Christ in this sense never saved anyone. Those who study the history of theology know that there was a Patristic theory explaining that Christ paid his ransom to the devil. Hugo Grotius expounded a governmental theory. The evangelist does not preach the Gospel unless he expounds the scriptural theory.

No evangelist can preach the Atonement without relying on a theory. The word *Atonement* itself is the name of and the result of a theory. The word *Satisfaction,* used earlier, and unfortunately replaced by the word Atonement, is also the name of and the result of a theory. It is the name of the scriptural theory. And unless this theory is preached, the Atonement, the Satisfaction, the Gospel is not preached. Therefore, we may say that Mr. Stott espouses a theory, that his theory is not scriptural, and that it is controversial. May few evangelists follow his advice.

More recently Mr. Stott has published a much less offensive book, *Our Guilty Silence* (Eerdmans, 1967). In the interval it seems that the author has read and profited by the publications of Dr. J. I. Packer (pp. 90, 102). Since this more recent book aims mainly at encouraging evangelistic effort, large sections are beyond reproach. Evangelism needs to be encouraged. Even doctrinally it contains several excellent statements. For example, "We are not to preach a vague Christ, but a precise and particular Christ, namely the Christ of the New Testament" (p. 31); and "If we now ask what Christ did to secure salvation for sinners, the chief answer is: He died" (p. 33); and "He gave himself as a ransom once" (p. 34). Mr. Stott even refers to the sentiment "impart a minimum of truth . . . without doctrinal formulation"—a sentiment he seems to have shared in his earlier book—but adds here "With this viewpoint the apostles would certainly have disagreed." On the next page he reinforces this excellent remark with the assertion, "To preach the gospel means preaching Christian dogma" (pp. 50, 51).

One must unfortunately note, however, that the *chief* point about Christ's ministry, namely his death, is not an adequate account of the Gospel; not even the better reference to his death as a ransom is sufficiently precise and particular. Neither the phrase "preaching Christian dogma" nor the most commendable observation that the Apostles did not approve of a mere minimum of truth without doctrinal formulation defines the extent of the message to be preached.

In spite of these improvements this more recent book repeats rather than retracts some of the most objectionable features of the earlier one. Perhaps the approval of Holman Hunt's *The Light of the World*, where Christ is portrayed as unable to enter the heart of man, may be passed off as the artistic taste and theological ignorance of an old pensioner (p. 82). But one cannot so shrug off Mr. Stott's plain statement that "the order of events to which the apostles commonly bear witness is that faith is antecedent to life. It is by believing that we live" (p. 104). That this assertion does not mean merely that the daily life I now live in the flesh, I live by the faith of the Son of God is very clear from the context. The question was, Does regeneration precede conversion? Calvinists argue that since man is dead in sin, he cannot repent and believe until he is born from above. This is what Mr. Stott quotes and denies. He conditions regeneration on a faith somehow produced before the sinner is raised from the dead.

To support his contention he says, "It is dangerous to argue from analogy and say 'dead men cannot....'" Mr. Stott ignores the fact that it was not the Calvinists who originated this analogy. The analogy is scriptural. But if anyone wants plain univocal speech, let him remember the words, "The carnal mind is enmity against God." This is not an analogy.

In addition to belittling scriptural analogy Mr. Stott's quotation refers to John 3:15, 16; 5:25; and 20:31. The first two verses hardly support the Arminian view. Nor does the last. John 20:31 reads, "But these are written that ye might believe that Jesus is the Christ, the Son of God; and that believing ye might have life through his name." If the last clause means that believing produces regeneration, then the first clause would have to mean that John's authorship produces faith. Both clauses are purpose clauses; they would have to be explained similarly. The verse can easily be translated, "These things are written . . . that believers may have life." The participial substantive points out the group of people who live. There is no way an Arminian can show by this verse that faith causes regeneration or that regeneration and faith are not simultaneous. The difficulty arises only because regeneration, like birth, is momentary, but faith continues throughout life.

The verse on which Mr. Stott puts most emphasis is John 5:25; at least he quotes it and not the others: "the dead will hear the voice of the Son of God, and those that hear will live" (p. 104). On the basis of these words the author asserts that faith antecedes regeneration and that it is dangerous to trust the scriptural analogy between death and sin. A reply to this argument is very easy to make. In my little book, *Biblical Predestination,* I have quoted nearly five hundred verses that form a background into which Mr. Stott's interpretation will not fit. Romans 3:11, 12, 18 say that "There is none that seeketh after God . . . There is none that doeth good . . . There is no fear of God before their eyes." Now faith is a seeking after God, at least it is something good, and it involves a pious fear of God. It must therefore follow regeneration, for Paul denies that these things are true of the unregenerate. These are only three of the five hundred verses. One other is particularly appropriate because it occurs in the immediate context, in fact it is the preceding verse, John 5:24, which says, "The one who hears my words . . . has passed from death to life." Hearing in the present tense is the evidence that the one who was dead became alive in the perfect tense and so remains alive forever.

This quotation is not a mere analogy, even a scriptural analogy, but a literal statement that life precedes hearing. An analogy might be Lazarus who heard Christ say, "Lazarus, come forth!" Lazarus had to have been resurrected a moment before he heard—unless one say his soul in paradise heard and came back. One sure thing—his decayed corpse did not hear. Or, if one wish an example of similar linguistic usage in a modern setting, one may suppose that a physician, speaking of babies, says, Those that breathe will live. Does this mean that breath produces life, that breath antecedes life, or simply that the baby to continue living must breathe?

It is instructive to note also the dilemma in which Mr. Stott gets tangled by his attempt to recognize the work of the Holy Spirit while maintaining his Arminian interpretations. On pages 108-109 he writes, " 'No one can come to me unless the Father draw him.' We need to hear much more in the Church of this 'no one can,' this natural inability of men to believe in Christ. . . . [To which I say, Amen.] Jesus also said, 'You are not willing to come . . .' The human mind finds it impossible neatly to resolve the tension between this 'cannot' and this 'will not.' " My comment is that Mr. Stott's inability to resolve this tension does not prove that some other mind cannot. Those who accept the clear Calvinistic sense of the scriptural texts find that the tension is imaginary.

In contrast with Mr. Stott's non-evangelical views I would like to commend to all readers the excellent statement of the Gospel made by J. I. Packer, pages 57-73 in his *Evangelism and the Sovereignty of God.* The title of the sub-section is "What is the Evangelistic Message?" Mr. Packer is very clear that it is not "Christ died for our sins . . . without . . . further elucidation." This is why he takes thirteen pages to summarize it. He apologizes for shortening it, as unfortunately it must be in a small book. The summary is divided into four parts. The first part is the thesis that the evangelistic message is a message about God. "It tells us who he is, what his character is, what his standards are, and what he requires of us, his creatures." Even in this opening sentence, we breathe a fresh, new atmosphere, full of sound theology, with the hope of reasonable elucidation. His second point is that the Gospel is a message about sin. After three pages on sin, Mr. Packer adds three sub-heads under sin: (i) "Conviction of sin is essentially an awareness of a wrong relationship with God; . . . (ii) Conviction of sin always involves conviction of sins. . . . (iii) Conviction of sin always includes conviction of sinfulness. . . ." His third point is "The Gospel is a message about Christ," under which he has the two sub-points, "(i) We must not present the person of Christ apart from his saving work. . . . (ii) We must not present the saving work of Christ apart from his person. . . ." Finally, the fourth point is, "The Gospel is a summons to faith and repentance." Here is a man who obviously knows a great deal about the Gospel. He wants the message proclaimed. He has the right ideas about evangelism; and it would do every Christian good to read his book.

There are nonetheless certain points on which I believe Mr. Packer to be woefully wrong. He is not wrong about the Gospel. But I believe he is wrong in evaluating the people who hear the Gospel and perhaps accept it, or seem to accept it. In defending the sovereignty of God, he appeals to Christian or apparently Christian experience and says that all Christians believe in prayer, and that a person who prays acknowledges God's sovereignty. He also says, "You have never for one moment supposed that the decisive contribution to your salvation was yours and not God's." He also says, "You pray for the conversion of others."

Now, it is clear that any Christian who prays for the conversion of others and who never for a moment thinks that his action was decisive admits, at least tacitly, the sovereignty of God. But there are so many in professedly Christian evangelistic services who do no such things. In Indianapolis, as I said a moment ago, I heard Billy Graham tell his audience not to pray for the conversion of those who had come forward, because not even God himself could help them. The decisive thing was their own choice. Mr. Packer knows the message, but I fear he does not realize the extent of the opposition.

There is another point at which I would like to suggest a correction of what Mr. Packer says. It seems to me that he goes astray because he imports into the religious argument an analogy from science, an analogy that science does not itself justify. Mr. Packer distinguishes between a *paradox,* which can be solved and explained by a little ingenuity, and an *antinomy,* which he says is insoluble. His scientific example is the two theories of light, the wave theory and the corpuscular theory, both of which scientists use, but which are mutually incompatible. Then Mr. Packer says that there are antinomies in the Bible. The antinomy between divine sovereignty and human responsibility is one such.

It seems to me that a misunderstanding of science at this point has led the author into a misunderstanding of the Bible. If the Bible contradicts itself, as clearly as the wave theory contradicts the corpuscular theory, we will be forced to abandon the Bible. No one in his right mind can believe contradictions. In fact, if the antinomy is as he says it is, God himself is faced with an insoluble puzzle. And if something is insoluble for God, then God cannot be trusted. Packer tells us that God has given us this antinomy and if he has given it to us, is that not enough? Cannot we trust God? The answer is that we cannot trust contradictions and insoluble antinomies, no matter who gives them to us. If someone told me to believe that the number two was both even and odd, I would conclude that this someone was not God. God, anyone I could think of as God, does not talk nonsense, and insoluble antinomies are nonsense. They are just as much nonsense as it would be to say that the path of a point equidistant from a given point has three right angles along it.

But if we see what modern science can do with its two theories of light, and if we pay just a little attention to sovereignty and responsibility, these unfortunate consequences never arise. The laws of science should not be considered as intended descriptions of natural motions. They should be considered as directions for operating in a physics laboratory. They are methods for producing desired results. This in brief is the theory of Operationalism, which I have defended in *The Philosophy of Science and Belief in God*. It is always possible to use either of two mutually exclusive methods for producing the same desired result. To cure milk fever in cows, one may use the antiseptic lugol, or one may use compressed air. Both work satisfactorily. Hence, in manipulating light, a physicist may use either one; or if for a particular purpose the two are not equally satisfactory, for lugol cannot do everything compressed air can do and vice versa, the physicist can use one for one purpose and the other for another.

As for sovereignty and responsibility, it is relatively easy to see that they are not antinomies. Sovereignty and free will would be an antinomy and contradiction; for sovereignty means that God controls all things, including our wills, and free will means that our wills are not controlled by God. This is a clear contradiction. Only an insane person could believe both of these. But responsibility does not mean free will. Responsibility means that God can demand of us a response. God can hold us to account. Far from conflicting with sovereignty, this is an exercise of sovereignty. If there were no sovereignty, if there were no superior to hold us accountable, there would be no responsibility. For further elucidations, see my small book on *Biblical Predestination*.*

Another but smaller booklet than J. I. Packer's *Evangelism*

_____

* Now called *Predestination*.

and the Sovereignty of God is Iain Murray's *The Invitation System,* published by The Banner of Truth Trust. Evangelism would flourish today if a thousand American ministers would read these two small books. Mr. Murray stresses preaching the Gospel. His opening words are, "An invariable characteristic of true preaching has been the assurance that the proclamation of the Gospel is the divinely ordained means for the conviction and conversion of sinners."

The booklet, however, deals chiefly with the deplorable practices in evangelistic services, which practices hinder the progress of or obscure the clarity of the Gospel. The particular practice singled out for examination is that of inviting members of the audience to come forward at the end of the sermon. Connected with this coming forward are an after-meeting, signing cards, and perhaps visiting the people in their homes after the campaign.

The method seems to have been invented by Charles Finney in the middle of the nineteenth century. Mr. Murray notes that it was unknown in Britain until recently. Now, anything Finney did or said is suspect, or worse. He was a disaster. Years and decades after his evangelistic campaigns he was still preventing men from believing the Gospel. Still, one cannot argue that because Finney stood on a platform, no evangelist should stand on a platform. Possibly even inviting the audience to walk down to the front could be a good thing.

It could of course be bad. It could be bad in itself—unlike standing on a platform; or it could be bad merely in some accidental aspects that happen to be widely used at present. Mr. Murray picks out several such. For example, the evangelist often leaves it unclear why a person should come forward. I have heard evangelists give such a wide invitation that virtually the whole audience could come forward. Those who wished to accept Christ, those who wanted a new experience, those who had doubts and perplexities, those who wanted the evangelist to pray for them—all come to the front! Then the next day's newspaper could give the number that responded.

Even if the invitation is more restricted, there are difficulties. Remarks Mr. Murray, "Is the walk forward an outward declaration of an inner saving decision already made by the hearer in his seat, just as an 'act of witness'? Why then are they told to 'come forward and *receive* Christ'?" The author describes in some detail the confusion observed in evangelistic services between receiving Christ and a public profession of having received him. There is Scriptural warrant for the latter; but none for receiving Christ by coming forward. Coming forward ought not to be explained as coming to receive Christ. To do so is like interpreting John 8:38 to mean that "continuing in the word" is the *method* by which one *becomes* a Christian, instead of the act of one who already is a Christian. Similarly John 15:8 does not say that fruit bearing is the *process* by which we *become* Christians. Coming forward in a service therefore may be a public profession of having become a Christian, but it cannot be understood as coming to Christ.

In a following section Mr. Murray examines certain psychological arguments. Evangelists use them to defend their methods. Non-Christians use them to reduce evangelism to the naturalistic power of mass appeal. He quotes Billy Graham's calling the attention of the audience to the hundreds coming forward, and claiming that "tens of thousands will have come to know Christ" in this manner.

The theology that underlies this use of an invitation is given by Harold J. Ockenga. He says, "Some reformed theologians teach that regeneration by the Holy Spirit precedes conversion. The evangelical position is that regeneration is conditioned upon repentance, confession, and faith." This is remarkable ignorance on Ockenga's part. It is not true that "some" Reformed theologians teach that regeneration precedes conversion. *All* Reformed theologians do. Second, Ockenga tries to exclude these Reformed theologians from the evangelical fold. He contrasts the Reformation theology with the "evangelical view." According to Ockenga therefore none of the Puritans was evangelical. To support his bad theology Ockenga relies on his ignorance of Greek grammar in his exegesis of Ephesians 2:8. He wants faith to be the result of human ability, an ability found in every man before regeneration; he does not want faith to be a gift from God.

When such unscriptural ideas are held, it is no wonder that the invitation to come forward is either confused or completely bad.

It does seem to me, however, that Mr. Murray has restricted his attention to one aspect or one form of "coming forward." His warnings against adulterating the Gospel with bad Greek and worse theology are well taken. Nevertheless, good theology and great clarity can make use of inviting people to come forward. The present writer insists that evangelism is preaching the Gospel; that a few sermons are inadequate; that as much elucidation as possible must be given. If this be so, then an evangelist, after having explained how Christ satisfied the justice of his Father because of man's disobedience to and depravity before God, and after having declared the Resurrection and its implications, can very well invite those who are interested to come forward and enter counseling sessions for the purpose of a clearer and a more extensive understanding. This is much more necessary now than it was in Britain before the time of Finney.

In those days many people heard the Gospel weekly. Some were catechized in their homes. Very few in Britain were as ignorant as today's American populace. If the people of that happier age needed instruction, the need is ten-fold greater now. Why cannot the method of coming forward be used to set up classes for Bible study? Cards could be signed: they could be signed as class cards in college, for admission to classes projected ahead of time and ready to receive the people. Thus when properly used the method of coming forward is just as good as the method of standing on a platform while preaching. The essential thing is the message preached.

The same principle applies to hillbilly singing. If it detracts from the message, it is bad. If it were used with a moderately well educated audience, with people who have some taste in music, it would so detract, by repelling them. On the other hand, I cannot agree with a friend of mine who says that good Reformed theology requires that only Bach should be used. Oh dear, no Mozart and not even Handel's *Messiah*! Personally I prefer good music, just as I prefer good grammar; but the Scripture does not specify what style of music must be used. As the Westminster Confession says, "there are some circumstances concerning the worship of God and government of the Church, common to human actions and societies, which are to be ordered by the light of nature and Christian prudence."

In conclusion, the Gospel is a message, a message that Mr. Packer and Mr. Murray understand very well and that some others do not. Evangelism is a matter of proclaiming that message. If the message is not proclaimed, all the hillbilly music in Kentucky and Tennessee will not make the service evangelistic. If the message is proclaimed, the accidents can be as they may; the effort is *ipso facto* evangelism.

Chapter Six

Faith

It is clear now that spiritual life does not depend on emotion. The Bible recognizes instances of emotion as they occasionally occur, but the connotation of the word *heart* in seventy-five per cent of the instances is intellect. It has also been made clear that the Gospel is a message, and as such is either true or false. The unregenerate man believes that the message, even if it contains some true statements, is basically false; the evangelist presents it as true. The latter asks the former to believe the message and pray that God will make him do so. Emotions have no essential part in any of this.

What then is faith? An old Protestant tradition analyzes faith into three parts whose Latin names are *notitia, assensus,* and *fiducia.* These words mean knowledge, assent, and trust. I would not deny that faith includes these three. Yet as an analysis the three-fold division of faith may be technically inadequate.

First, knowledge or understanding is at least ordinarily regarded as a part of faith. The Lutherans may deny that it is always so. Their argument is that God's decision of justification is connected with an individual person by means of faith alone. Since, now, we have good reason to believe that some or even all who die in infancy are saved, and quite likely idiots, freaks, and mentally deformed persons, both of which groups are incapable of understanding any message at all, it follows, say the Lutherans, that they must have a faith devoid of knowledge.

Faith is essential; knowledge is not. Therefore infants can exercise faith.

The Reformed theologians reply that the Epistle to the Romans and the preaching of the Gospel are addressed to normal individuals. These persons who are not naturally incapacitated in their mental functions are to be justified by faith. But since the Gospel presumably cannot penetrate the mind of an infant or the no-mind of an idiot, God in mercy treats them as exceptions to the normal rule and saves them, on the basis of Christ's sacrifice indeed, but without faith. As the Westminster Confession puts it, "Elect infants, dying in infancy, are regenerated and saved by Christ through the Spirit, who worketh when, and where, and how he pleaseth. So also are all other elect persons, who are incapable of being outwardly called by the ministry of the Word" (X, iii).

The Reformed position therefore makes understanding an essential part of faith, even at the cost of denying that infants can believe. Aside from infants the preaching of a message would make no sense unless the auditors were supposed to know what was being said. This is why missionaries must work hard to learn a foreign language and try to speak it without an American accent. This is why the Apostles on the day of Pentecost spoke in tongues. The Elamites and the dwellers in Mesopotamia heard the message in their own language. If the message were not supposed to be understood, there would be no need to learn Arabic or Chinese. One could simply speak American slang or quote the Bible in the King James Version.

Understanding, therefore, is a prerequisite to faith. It is impossible to believe what one does not understand. The evangelist or missionary must spare no pains to help his prospective convert to understand the message.

Just how much has to be understood is difficult to measure. Obviously a child of ten cannot understand as much as a highly educated adult; yet God regenerates some children. Does it follow that God will regenerate a highly educated adult if he understands no more than a child? Some individuals and some churches have tried to set down minimum requirements. They have tried to separate the few sentences in the Bible that are essential from all the rest that is unessential. One can see how these people become interested in such an attempt, but one cannot see any Biblical recommendation of such an attempt. Christ commanded us to teach all the things he taught; Paul was guiltless of his auditors' blood because he had declared all the counsel of God; and many other passages condemn ignorance and recommend knowledge. In Scripture there is no minimum.

Some theologians try to explain this situation by insisting that truth is organic. Minimum statements are not inert building blocks which when combined with other building blocks can be arranged into a building. Rather, a truth or proposition is like a seed, and when ingested it grows into a full plant in the mind. Hence, say these theologians, any Biblical statement, or at least some Biblical statements contain the complete Gospel as a seed contains the complete plant. Unfortunately for these theologians, their analogy, though it be a beautiful illustration, is intellectually vacuous. Illustrations are usually if not always deceptive; and to say that a proposition is like a seed that grows means nothing and throws no light on the nature of faith.

Since the position this present writer defends places such great emphasis on propositions—on an intelligible message composed of sentences—it would seem that he above all writers should indicate which propositions are essential and which are not. No one can understand all the propositions in the Bible, or at least no one actually understands all that the Bible implies. What then are the facts essential to salvation?

The thief on the cross very obviously understood only a little. Is not this little, if we can discover it, sufficient for an evangelist's sermons? Well, the thief called Jesus Lord. And Romans 10:9 says that those who acknowledge Jesus as Lord shall be saved. Here if anywhere is the essential proposition. Nothing else—except belief in the Resurrection—is necessary. Maybe the Resurrection is not necessary, for the thief did not know that. Furthermore, as other references in this book mention, the devils believe there is one God, they even believe that Jesus is the Son of God, but by some twist of demonic mentality, they do not confess him as Lord. Have not we therefore found the irreducible minimum?

The answer is, No. The reason for this negative answer lies in the necessity of understanding the proposition. It is a matter of intellectual apprehension. There are many who in that day will say to Christ, Lord, Lord. And he will profess, I never knew you. Thus, clearly, a verbal profession of Lord is not saving faith. One must understand what the term Lord means. Further, as has already been pointed out, the name Jesus must be correctly apprehended. Confess that the Jesus of Strauss, Renan, or Schweitzer is Lord, and you will go to hell. "Jesus is Lord" therefore is not a minimum that means nothing else.

The thief on the cross knew or at least said that Jesus was Lord. Did he know anything else? How did he learn anything? Of all people, meeting Jesus for the first time on the cross, he had little opportunity to learn. And a cross is neither the best pulpit for preaching nor the best pew for listening. But perhaps the thief knew more than most people give him credit for.

In the first place one must not assume that this was the first time he had seen and heard Jesus. An enterprising criminal gets around. He knows where crowds gather. This thief may have heard one of Jesus' sermons. Of course, we cannot be sure he did. Yet we cannot be sure he did not. Since the Gospels do not say, one can neither assume his ignorance nor his knowledge;

though I would think it more probable that he knew some-thing.

But not to rely on guesses, let us consider the few painful hours on the cross. The thief knew the charge on which the Romans had crucified Jesus. He could read it above the cross: Jesus of Nazareth, the King of the Jews. Couldn't he read? Then he heard the horrible crowds screaming it. He also knew that Jesus claimed to be the Messiah, the Christ, the Son of God. The rulers were deriding him: "He saved others, let him save himself, if he be Christ, the chosen of God. . . . If thou be the King of the Jews, save thyself." The other thief knew this: "One of the malefactors . . . railed on him, saying, If thou be the Christ, save thyself and us." The thief had also heard Jesus say, "Father forgive them, for they know not what they do."

So he turned to Jesus and said, "Lord, remember me when thou comest into thy kingdom."

The thief was not a systematic theologian. There were many propositions he did not know. But he knew he was being punished justly for his sins; he knew Jesus was innocent. He was impressed and convinced by Jesus' demeanor. So he said, not merely said, but confessed Jesus as Lord. He may not have known much, but he knew more than some evangelists give him credit for.

For such reasons as these the idea of a minimum faith must be dropped as unbiblical. The evangelist is unbiblical who decides to preach only a little bit of God's revelation. Granted that no preacher can cover the entire Bible in one sermon, nevertheless he should not decide on principle to omit certain themes. He should in many sermons try to explain all he can. "All he can" no doubt should be limited by what the audience or the prospect can understand. One of the worst principles imaginable was expressed by a very popular but very stupid evangelist in Canada who said, No one has the right to hear the

Gospel twice until everybody has heard it once. Another man of similar sentiments boasted that he had preached on five continents. But more than likely the poor natives in the Andes or the Himalayas understood nothing at all when the preacher gave them one sermon and then ran off to another continent.

The Gospel is a message to be understood. Knowledge is the first and an essential part of faith.

But though it is essential, knowledge or understanding alone is not faith. A man may know and understand the Gospel message and yet not believe it. A professor of philosophy knows and understands many systems of philosophy, but obviously he cannot believe them all. He may accept one, but the others he knows without accepting. Therefore a second essential part of faith is acceptance or assent.

The explicit notion of assent seems to have entered philosophic discussions through the Stoics. Their theory of knowledge Zeno "illustrated with a piece of action. When he stretched out his fingers and showed the palm of his hand, 'perception,' said he, 'is a thing like this.' Then when he had a little closed his fingers, 'Assent is like this.' Afterwards when he had completely closed his hand and held forth his fist, that he said was comprehension. . . . But when he brought his left hand against his right and with it took a firm and tight hold of his fist, he said that knowledge was of that character and that was what none but a wise man possessed" (Cicero, *Academics,* II, XI vii).

Of course illustrations explain nothing. Terms should be defined rather than illustrated. Now, in the illustration Zeno, since he and the Stoics were materialists, was thinking of perceiving a physical object. He was not thinking of believing a proposition. Therefore his notion of assent is not too useful in Christian theology. Furthermore, in the latter, "comprehension," when it is said that God is incomprehensible, means something much further up the scale from Zeno's comprehension. Once more, if Zeno had been talking about propositions, our "knowledge" or "understanding" would be far down the scale from his.

After the Stoics, the Christian philosopher Augustine made use of assent. Augustine was not much interested in physical objects; his theory, on one reputable interpretation, does not even speak of concepts; he clearly puts great emphasis on truth, and assent is the voluntary decision to believe an understood proposition.

This Augustinian view continued in Christian philosophy or theology. The word *notitia*, used by Christians in discussing faith, means simply an idea, a notion, a concept, or, as above, the understanding of what a proposition means. *Assent* means the voluntary act of believing the proposition to be true. I understand or know what Spinoza means by saying God is nature; but I do not assent to it. I also know or understand the meaning of the proposition, "Christ died." That is not hard to understand and everybody assents to it. Further, I understand the proposition "Christ died for our sins." So do many other people; but they do not all assent to it; they do not all believe it. I do.

This matter of assent, however, can be seriously misunderstood. In one discussion an otherwise competent theologian took assent to refer to a verbal and public profession of faith. He then noted that such a profession can be and sometimes is hypocritical. Therefore, he concluded, assent itself, or with understanding, is not faith.

This argument depends on a misunderstanding of assent. Assent can never be hypocritical, for it is the voluntary act of according belief to a given proposition. There need be no verbal and public manifestation. Assent is an inner act of will.

Whether I can know that another person has assented to something, or not, is a difficult problem. The safest thing is to say that one can never know about another person. This is one reason why Presbyterians and Baptists disagree. Baptists, or many of them, hold that the church should receive as members only those who have been regenerated. This presupposes that the present church members can know the applicant to have been regenerated. Presbyterians, on the contrary, hold that God alone can discern the hearts of men. Therefore the elders receive an applicant into membership on the basis of a credible profession, including a life free from gross, observable sin. The Presbyterians are often mistaken and receive people who later show no signs of being Christian. But I suppose the Baptists too make mistakes and sometimes accept a hypocrite, a modernist, or some other unbeliever.

A most interesting, informative, and unfortunate example came to my attention some years ago. There was a very lively, energetic fundamentalist minister in the neighborhood who had increased his church membership from about forty to four or five hundred within ten years. I was discussing with him the nature of faith. I spoke of assent to propositions, and quoted the well known verse, "If thou shalt confess with thy mouth that Jesus is Lord, and believe in thy heart that God raised him from the dead, thou shalt be saved." Oh, no, he replied. You cannot be saved that way at all. At any rate, no one knows what the Bible means, but God has given us (the ministers or the people?) the ability to discern the hearts of men, and we know whether they are regenerated, and so we receive them.

A few years after this conversation, ugly rumors began to trouble his church. The officers at first discounted them, as they should. But the rumors got worse and the evidence began to grow. Half the church walked out and formed a new congregation because the officers were too slow in administering discipline. The rumors and evidence were true. The fundamentalist minister who could see the hearts of men deserted his wife and children and went to live openly with another woman in the same city.

Was he, is he regenerate? Did he ever assent to the proposition, Jesus is Lord? I do not know, but at the moment it does not seem so. It may be so. Christians "may, through the temptations of Satan and the world, the prevalency of corruption remaining in them, and the neglect of the means of their preservation, fall into grievous sins; and for a time continue therein; whereby they incur God's displeasure, and grieve his Holy Spirit . . ." but nonetheless "can neither totally nor finally fall away from the state of grace; but shall certainly persevere therein to the end, and be eternally saved" (Westminster Confession, XVII, iii and iv). But whether the particular case, the man in question, was ever a Christian or not, I do not know.

Protestants usually assert that Romanists make faith and salvation a matter of assent; the most frequent expression is that the Romanists make faith a matter of "bare" assent. It is common to declaim against "mere" intellectual faith. *Bare* and *mere* are of course pejorative adjectives, *i.e.,* weasel words. It is unfortunate that many or most Protestant discussions on this subject, either in textbooks or encyclopedias, do not define their terms and explain what is meant. Assent, as has been seen, can be taken in several ways. Orthodox Protestants have always said that faith must produce good works. Faith, or what passes for faith, or what some people call faith, is dead without works. If this is what is meant by speaking of "mere" or "bare" assent, of course it is quite true. But I suspect that this is not what is meant.

At any rate, Protestantism has insisted that in addition to understanding the message, and in addition to believing the message, there must be *fiducia,* trust. Well, of course, there must be trust. I am not sure that even the Romanists deny this. But the fact that there must be trust does not guarantee the analysis of faith into understanding, assent, and trust.

Suppose I were a budding botanist and wished to classify plants. I might say that plants are divided into the rose family (including apple trees), the lily family, and asparagus. If I made this classification, the budding botanist would die in the bud. Of course, asparagus is part of the plant kingdom; but asparagus is a subdivision of the lily family. Therefore the threefold analysis is faulty. The second heading already includes asparagus.

Plausibility is gained for the division of faith into knowledge, belief, and trust by an illustration. I read the financial report of a bank. This is *notitia*. I believe that the information is true. This is *assent*. But I do not have faith in the bank, until I deposit some money in it. This is *trust*.

Now, illustrations are always useless and usually deceptive. In the first place, there are many banks I trust, even though I have no checking accounts in them. These other banks are just as sound as the one I use; only I do not have enough money to support two checking accounts. I would not hesitate to open a checking account in any one of them, were it convenient. It is not that I do not trust them—I just cannot conveniently use two banks.

Furthermore, the deception in the illustration lies in the fact that it tries to make faith a matter of some physical action. You read the financial report; you decide that the bank is sound; you then deposit money in it. But this latter physical action has no counterpart in a purely mental, internal, non-physical situation. We hear the Gospel message. We believe it. What else is there to do? If we confess that Jesus is Lord, we are saved. Of course, good works are to follow: but those who insist on *fiducia* as something in addition to assent do not locate faith in these external good works. Faith is completely mental. It is not physical. Why then is not trust one kind of assent? If it is not asparagus, maybe it is bellwort. Naturally saving faith is not assent to the proposition that two and two make four. There are many acts of assent that are not faith in Christ. But this indubitable fact does not imply that faith in Christ is not assent.

Here a little more history of the subject should be inserted, for the topic was an important one to the early Reformers and the somewhat later Puritans. These latter, like Calvin, considered faith to be an activity of the "whole man." But their dependence on the faculty psychology of their day betrayed them. This is one example among many of the confusions a Christian can fall into by taking for Gospel truth a contemporary scientific theory that the scientists will inevitably repudiate a century or even a decade later. The faculty psychology talked as if man "had" a will and "had" an intellect. These were looked upon somewhat as entities, even independent entities in a certain sense. It was they which acted, rather than the "whole man." The Puritans therefore alternately stressed intellect and will.

A theologian whom Jonathan Edwards studied, Shepard by name, stressed intellect. William Ames said, "Saving knowledge . . . follows the act of will and depends upon it." Solomon Stoddard, Edwards' grandfather, noted that the understanding and the will "are not two things, but one and the same soul [with] two several ways of working." John Locke, not one of the best theologians, but one whom Edwards studied carefully, also repudiated faculty psychology.

Edwards made use of Locke's "simple ideas" to explain faith as the sense of taste. No man can teach another what the taste of a peanut is. To get this knowledge, and for both Locke and Edwards this is knowledge, one must taste the peanut for himself. Perry Miller, excellent scholar though he is, is mistaken in understanding this tasting experience as a "feeling" divorced from knowledge. And another author is wildly wrong in asserting that Edwards was anti-intellectual.

In trying to explain how God acts in producing faith, Stoddard had taught that God operates directly on the understanding, but mediately on the will. Jonathan Edwards tries to avoid a temporal sequence of acts in faith (of the human acts in the first instance but by implication of the divine acts also) and asserts that they penetrate each other.

Much of this is hard to understand or even devoid of sense. Although great emphasis is laid on faith's being an act of the "whole man," this very true idea is completely useless in distinguishing the act of faith from other acts. In the faculty psychology—though even here with some inconsistency perhaps—it was possible to identify one act as the act of the will, a second as the act of the intellect, and a third as an act of the whole man. But if we insist, as we do, on the unity of the person, every act, even tasting a peanut, is an act of the whole man. There is no other agent. Therefore this characteristic of every human act is useless for distinguishing faith from anything else.

Likewise, when Edwards says that several human acts, all relating to faith, interpenetrate, he does not advance the explanation of faith. Nor does it seem to me at all advantageous to deny a temporal sequence of a sort. At least an act of understanding precedes and continues in actual faith.

Recently considerable secular attention has been directed to Jonathan Edwards. Philosophers have discovered that he was a man of great intellectual ability, of wide philosophical interests, and was a landmark in American thought. What has always been commonplace knowledge for the spiritual heirs of the Puritans and the Covenanters now appears as scholarly research in academic publications. It is interesting how a secular author like Conrad Cherry in *The Theology of Jonathan*

Edwards can with learned profundity state some simple evangelical principles and at the same time stumble into gross misrepresentations of his sources. On page 47 he quotes Francis Turretin on the work of God's Spirit in producing faith. Turretin naturally refers to the Holy Spirit as "he," a person; but in spite of the actual quotation on the page, Cherry refers to the Spirit as "it." The same author misinterprets Edwards' view of Scripture by trying to cast it in terms of contemporary dialectical theology, thus vitiating his exposition. This lack of spiritual perceptiveness, in fact this lack of intellectual acuity, vitiates many so-called scholarly books written by secular authors.

The Puritans themselves are not altogether blameless, either. One great difficulty in the writers on this subject is a tendency toward literary flourish, figures of speech, inexact terminology, and a paucity of definitions. One example is Thomas Manton, whom Jonathan Edwards explicitly opposed.

Thomas Manton, one of the Puritan writers, in his commentary on James, chapter two, verse nineteen, says that faith is not bare assent. Beyond bare assent, there must be "consent." And presumably there must be "consent" because faith is not merely a work of the understanding, but also a work of the heart. This is not at all satisfactory. If Manton wishes to add an extra element to the analysis, and to assent add consent, he should state the meaning of this new word. Ordinarily we should assume that he uses the term assent in its historical sense. He does not inform us that he is changing the meaning of assent. Then, if he wishes to point out something else, he should say explicitly what it is. But he does not; he merely uses another word. Really it is only a play on words. He reminds me of a certain professor of philosophy who dislikes deduction. To solve his problems he recommends adduction. This is a play on words. Anyone who has had a course in logic knows what deduction is. He can work out implications according to the rules. And if a person has not had a course in logic, he can still instinctively work out his problems by the same method. He may make a few false steps. He will not be so efficient and methodical. But he will finally use the same method. Adduction, however, is not a method at all. It has no rules. To appeal to it in solving problems, or in talking about solving problems, is to substitute a word for methodical thought. So too, consent is simply a word that happens to rhyme with assent. It means nothing.

In the same passage Manton also distinguishes between understanding and the "heart." It has already been seen that the term *heart* as used in the Bible is three-quarters of the time the intellect. The other instances are divided about two to one between will and emotion. Faith certainly involves an act of will. It is the decision to believe what one understands. Whether this is saving faith or only faith in the bank downtown, depends on what statement or statements are believed.

It would seem therefore that the analysis of faith into understanding, belief, and trust is a faulty analysis. It resembles the division of plants into the rose family, the lily family, and asparagus. The reason is that trust is a case of belief or assent. Therefore it is the duty of the evangelist to present the message, the object of belief; to present it so clearly that it can be understood. And then he must pray that God would make the hearer willing to believe, or more simply and accurately, make him believe. It is God alone who can take away their heart or mind of stone, and give them a mind of flesh, renew their wills, and by his almighty power determine them to that which is good, effectually drawing them to Jesus Christ, so that they come willingly, being made willing by his grace (paraphrased from the Westminster Confession, X i).

This clear statement is far superior to some of the involved

Puritan explanations of how the Holy Spirit can work faith, *i.e.* produce faith in a man's mind. Some of the Puritans, wrongly no doubt, have been interpreted to mean that the Spirit so unites himself to a man that the man is almost deified. How God gives a man faith is very easily explained. God gives a dead sinner faith just the way Jesus made dead Lazarus come out of the tomb. Just as God said, Let there be light, and there was light. That is all the *how* there is. It is an act of omnipotence: the exceeding greatness of his power to us-ward who believe according to the working of his mighty power which he wrought in Christ when he raised him from the dead.

Since the nature of faith is such an important subject, and since some theologians may think that I have departed from historic Protestantism in making faith a "mere" intellectual exercise, I shall add a section on Charles Hodge's view of faith. The aim is not to set forth Charles Hodge fully and accurately. Not that I intend to misrepresent him, either. My procedure is to show that a considerable amount of his material confirms the analysis above and offers no support for his different conclusion. Those who are interested in a fuller view of Hodge can easily find his *Systematic Theology,* Volume III, and read the lengthy section on pages 41-113, if they want it all.

Hodge opens his discussion by saying, "The first conscious exercise of the renewed soul is faith." This remark is to be most firmly accepted against all Arminian misrepresentations of man and the Bible. The difficulty in discussing faith, says Hodge, arises partly from the nature of the subject and partly from the variety of definitions given to it.

The first question therefore is, What is faith? "What is the psychological nature of the act or state of mind which we designate faith or belief?" This matter of definition is most important. It was necessary in an earlier chapter to define emotion, at least as best we could. Here the question is, What is faith? It was in answer to this question concerning the psychology of faith that the traditional answer was given: *notitia, assensus,* and *fiducia.* To proceed now, one may note that Hodge asks, what is faith or belief? This implied identity between faith and belief is one of several points in Hodge that support my conclusion about assent. It offers no support to, and may even prove inconsistent with Hodge's different conclusion. Even more, Hodge not only says "faith or belief," he adds, "Faith in the widest sense of the word is assent to the truth, or the persuasion of the mind that a thing is true." If this is the widest sense, then it seems necessary that any narrower sense should still be assent. It would be a certain type of assent, a species within a genus, but it would still be assent to the truth.

The next sentence is, "In ordinary popular language we are said to believe whatever we regard as true." This sentence again confirms my point, but Hodge begins to diverge. He says, "The primary element of faith is trust." Here apparently an undefined *fiducia,* the asparagus perhaps, enters the picture. Yet he is able to continue, *"Credo mihi;* trust me, rely on my word." Does this not suggest that trust in a person is assent to what he says?

In a few lines there comes the sub-head, "The Primary Idea of Faith is Trust." Still, commendably, Hodge connects trust with truth. "The primary idea of truth is that which is trustworthy." I am not so sure that the *primary* idea of truth is trust; but surely a truth can be trusted. Could not one conclude then that to trust a truth means to assent to it?

Hodge quotes Augustine: *"Credere, nihil aliud est, quam cum assension cogitare."* Wonderful! To believe is nothing other than to think with assent. This Augustinian position I shall uphold, though Hodge veers away from it.

An indication of withdrawal from the path of truth, assent, and belief is the sub-head, "Faith, Not a Voluntary Conviction."

Above Hodge had said that "faith in the widest sense of the word is assent." Here he denies it: Faith is not a voluntary conviction. His argument is extremely confused. If, he says, the wide sense of voluntary is used, then it "includes every operation of the mind not purely intellectual." This seems to place sensation, emotion, and even pain within the volitional. But if volition is so widened, is there any reason to exclude intellectual action? Does not one study, read, think voluntarily? More voluntarily than he senses or emotes. One cannot follow Hodge in this paragraph.

If, however, we do not use the wide sense of *voluntary*—though Hodge never said precisely what that wide sense is—and if we use the narrower sense that he calls "self-determination," then, concludes Hodge, when we believe a truth, it is because we choose to; and if we reject the proposition, it is because we will to disbelieve it. Hodge seems to think that this is a *reductio ad absurdum*. He seems unable to credit the notion that one can choose to believe or not to believe.

But why is this absurd? Suppose the proposition is "David was King of Israel." Or, "Napoleon reached Moscow." Each of these has some evidence in its favor. But often evidence, witnesses, and historical documents are mistaken. Shall I believe them in this case? The evidence does not compel belief; but I may choose to believe, or I may choose not to believe. Contrary to Hodge's opinion, this seems to me to be precisely what happens.

The great theologian's argument is further vitiated by a strange merging of volition and feeling or emotion. Under this heading, "Faith, Not a Voluntary Conviction," he concedes "it is true not only that faith in many cases is inseparable from feeling, but also that feeling has much influence in determining our faith." This is beside the point. Whether faith is assent and voluntary conviction cannot be settled by references to feelings or emotions. Yet apparently Hodge thinks so. After giving examples of instances of faith connected with feeling, he strives to make his point by saying, "But it is not true of all kinds of even religious faith." Then follow a few examples. After these Hodge continues, "If we turn to other than religious truths it is still more apparent that faith is not necessarily a voluntary assent of the mind. A man may hear of something repugnant to his feelings . . . but the testimony may . . . force conviction." The whole argument is that belief can sometimes occur without *feeling*, therefore belief is not *assent*. This argument is the wildest of nonsequiturs.

Along the road Hodge seems to intimate (and everyone may read him to see if this is so) that sometimes evidence for historical statements is so compelling that no voluntary assent is necessary. "A man can hardly be found who does not believe that the Israelites dwelt in Egypt, escaped from bondage, and took possession of the land of Canaan." Well, I once met a Jewish rabbi who denied the existence of Moses; and many scholars in Hodge's own day denied the existence of the Hittites. But perhaps the evidence of the Exodus is compelling. Yet this evidence did not compel Wellhausen. He did not believe that anything in the Pentateuch was true. Twentieth century historiography is much clearer than nineteenth century historiography that evidence is never compelling. Even if it were, belief would still be voluntary, the volition being caused by the evidence. In actual cases the volition is caused by something other than the evidence.

Coming closer to saving faith, instead of faith in general, Hodge constructs an ingenious but completely fallacious argument. A man dead in sin, Hodge notes, cannot believe the Gospel. "This inability to believe arises from the state of his mind. But this state of mind lies below the will. It cannot be determined or changed by the exercise of any voluntary power."

Now, although lying below the will is a meaningless phrase, and although the man dead in sin sins voluntarily, the rest of the statement is true. The man dead in sin cannot exercise voluntary faith. This is good Calvinism. He cannot by an act of his will change his position before God. The trouble is that Hodge draws from it the wrong conclusion. "On these grounds," he says, "the definition of faith, whether as generic or religious, as a voluntary assent to truth, must be considered unsatisfactory." The argument is a glaring fallacy. Hodge says that belief is not assent because here is a man who cannot believe. Of course, he cannot believe. Neither can he assent. How can an instance of non-belief prove that belief, when it does occur, is not voluntary? What is needed for saving faith is God's gracious act of giving him the power to will. When God gives him this power, he will assent, believe, and exercise faith. Faith indubitably is the gift of God. It is the gift of voluntary assent. That an unregenerate man cannot believe does not contradict any of this. Hodge's argument therefore, with its insistence that man is dead in sin and cannot will to believe, fails to prove the sub-head that faith is not a voluntary conviction.

It is not useful to reproduce every paragraph in Hodge. Many of them do not discuss assent. One or two more do. A few pages later Hodge quotes a number of men who say that faith is a conviction of truth founded on testimony. Several of these men use the word *assent.* Hodge ignores the *assent* and stresses the *testimony.* But the two concepts are not antithetical. Testimony is presented to someone. An account of an event is given to him, or the message of the Gospel. To this testimony he assents. Hodge thinks that testimony excludes voluntary assent; but why he thinks so is too difficult to guess. Hodge is really insisting on the necessity of revelation for saving faith. Most assuredly revelation is necessary. Believing or assenting to it is equally necessary.

After a good many pages, on which interesting aspects of faith are discussed, Hodge again has a sub-head, "Religious Faith More than Simple Assent" (p. 89), under which he opposes the idea that faith is purely an intellectual exercise. Now, let it be made clear again that the thesis defended in this small book insists that understanding the meaning of the Atonement is not saving faith, or any kind of faith. Assent to the proposition, belief of the proposition, is essential. Bellarmin, whom Hodge quotes, distinguishes between Romish doctrines and what he calls heresy by accusing the heretics of insisting on the will: *Siquidem illi fidem collcant in voluntate (seu in corde) dum fiduciam esse definiunt.* Latin makes the argument much more profound. The present author does not agree with Bellarmin. Volition is essential. It may also be true and somewhat confusing that there is a difference between *understanding* as here used and *intellect* as Bellarmin and probably Hodge use it. Hodge rightly complains that the Catholic interpretation of *intellect* implies that faith is not necessarily connected with salvation. A man may have true faith and yet perish. But though we hold that true faith is necessarily connected with salvation, we as Protestants must agree with the Romanists that faith as they define it, apart from assent, is not necessarily connected with salvation. On the soteriology Hodge is correct, but his argument has no effect on the status of assent.

The further one goes into the history of the theories of faith, the more complicated the subject becomes. Yet the matter is not only interesting, it is important also. Hodge, shortly after the last quoted passage, says, "Protestants with one voice maintain that the faith which is connected with salvation is not a mere intellectual exercise." Here is a complication. Hodge rejects the Romish view that located faith in the intellect. For reasons analyzed above he also refuses to locate faith in the will, as Bellarmin said Protestants do. Then where does Hodge locate faith? In the emotions? Logically that is the only place left. But no doubt this is not what Hodge intended. He actually continues by quoting Calvin, who in the *Institutes* III, ii, 8 says that the Romanists "maintain faith to be mere assent." Here is another complication. Bellarmin says that Catholics place faith in the intellect, not in the will; Calvin says Catholics make faith purely volitional. Then Calvin continues by insisting that faith is not the product of man's unaided powers. This, true as it is, has no bearing on assent. Yet Calvin in just another line seems to require assent, for he says, "The assent which we give to the Divine word . . . is from the heart rather than the head, and from the affections rather than from the understanding. For which reason it is called 'the obedience of faith,' . . . It is an absurdity to say that faith is formed by the addition of a pious affection to an assent of the mind; whereas even this assent consists in a pious affection. . . . Faith consists in a knowledge of Christ."

In this quotation from Calvin, note the emphasis on assent. Very good; and both against the late Arminians and with Calvin against the Romanists, this assent and faith are not products of our unaided efforts. The Spirit must make us willing. But the willing is assent.

I regret that Calvin, a giant among pygmies, said that assent comes from the heart and not from the head. This distinction is unscriptural; the Bible nowhere opposes heart to head, for it does not mention this "head." Naturally assent comes from the heart because all psychological actions of a person come from the heart. There is nothing else for them to come from.

Aside from this unfortunate slip, Calvin proceeds to say that assent is the obedience of faith. Clearly obedience is a matter of volition. Assent then is an act of will. No pious additions are necessary, for the assent itself is already pious.

It is amazing that so many writers who profess to be devout, and who are reputed so to be, fulminate against the assent of the mind, especially against the mind, and continue to insist that faith is not an intellectual exercise. Once again let it be said that understanding or intellect apart from belief and assent is not faith. But this is not what these anti-intellectuals mean. They wish to exclude faith from both the intellect and the will. It will then be an emotion. As such, faith is divorced from belief in the Gospel message.

That their objections to the intellect are unscriptural can be seen, in many passages to be sure, but for example in II Corinthians 4:2-6. Here the wicked are described as "handling the word of God deceitfully;" or, better, as adulterating or changing the message. They alter its intellectual content. Contrary to these are the saints, who manifest the truth. They make the truth clear and evident. They commend themselves to men by their attachment to the truth. Satan has blinded the minds of the unbelievers; he has blinded the thoughts of those who do not have faith. These men do not have the light of the Gospel message. Its truth and perhaps even its meaning do not dawn on them. To the elect, however, God has sent the light of day, the clear vision, the accurate knowledge of his glory. This knowledge is our knowledge of Jesus Christ.

To be noted in these verses is the function of the mind, the intellect, the truth, the cognitive content of the message.

Charles Hodge himself (p. 91) indicates where the source of some of the trouble lies. After quoting the Heidelberg Catechism, Faith "is not merely a certain knowledge" etc., he remarks that "the Scriptures do not make the sharp distinction between the understanding, the feelings, and the will, which is common in our day. A large class of our inward acts and states are so complex as to be acts of the whole soul, and not exclusively of any one of its faculties."

. Here one may suspect that the so-called faculty psychology of an earlier day has confused the theologians, who should have learned the unity of personality from the Biblical material. Hodge too, in the last sentence of the quotation, seems to posit separate faculties, of which at least some simple acts are the products. One should hold, rather, that every act is an act of the whole soul; *i.e.* every act is the act of the person. But the acts differ. The present discussion, although it has dismissed feeling and emotion as irrelevant, distinguishes between understanding the meaning of a proposition and assent to its truth. But both these different acts are acts of the same unitary person. Hodge is quite right in saying that the situation as a whole is more complicated than supposed. Even the intellectual work of coming to understand a sentence requires assent and volition. It does not require assent to the truth of the sentence in question; but it requires a voluntary act of attention, and assent to the truth of other propositions by which its meaning is uncovered. One of the important points to keep in mind is the object of assent in different contexts. The person who does not assent to the Gospel, the persecutor Saul for example, must assent to propositions regarding the Hebrew or Greek usage of the word *Lord*, if he is to understand "Jesus is Lord," and react with a persecutor's zeal. This point is immediately useful in Hodge.

Hodge continues, "There is a distinction to be made between faith in general and saving faith. If we take that element of faith which is common to every act of believing; if we understand by it the apprehension of a thing as true and worthy of confidence, whether a fact of history or of science, then it may be said that faith in its essential nature is intellectual or intelligent assent."

With this of course the present writer agrees completely; and it is a major concession by Hodge to the position here defended.

Hodge, however, continues, "But if the question be, What is the act or state of mind which is required in the Gospel, when we are commanded to believe, the answer is very different."

How can it be *very* different? If faith generically is intelligent assent, every species of faith must be also. After all, asparagus is a lily. It has differentia, to be sure. Asparagus is not bellwort; but it is a lily.

Contrary to this relationship between genus and species, or between concept and instance, Hodge says, "To believe that Christ is 'God manifest in the flesh,' is not the mere intellectual conviction that no one, not truly divine, could be and do what Christ was and did; for this conviction the demoniacs avowed; but it is to receive him as our God."

Note the fallacy that Hodge falls into. His argument is: Faith is not assent because the demoniacs assented to the proposition that Jesus is the Son of God. This argument does not prove that faith is not assent; it only proves that assent to the proposition that Jesus is the Son of God is not saving faith. When one says that faith is assent, one does not mean that assent to just any proposition is saving faith. In James 2:19 it says that the devils believe that there is one God. Assent to the proposition that there is one God is not saving faith. Still, for all of this, saving faith can be assent to another proposition. Obviously assent to propositions regarding a bank's sound financial structure is not saving faith. Nor is assent to the proposition that David was King of Israel. It may seem strange at first sight that belief that Jesus is the Son of God is not saving faith; but the reference to the demoniacs makes this clear. Hodge has confused the psychology of belief with the object of belief. The distinguishing feature between faith in general and saving faith is a distinction in their objects, not in the psychology. The distinguishing feature cannot possibly be a denial to the species of its generic character. Faith in Christ and faith in a bank are equally faith, with whatever characteristic mental actions are necessary. The difference does not lie in the action of assent, but in the object assented to. The difference is the difference between Christ and a bank. It is a difference that concerns *what* is believed, not *how* belief takes place.

There is another fallacy in Hodge, or if not a fallacy, at least a misdirected analysis. Recall that he said, "The primary idea of truth is that which is trustworthy." It is thus that Hodge tries to shift from belief, which is too closely allied with assent, to a *fiducia* that is not assent. Perhaps Hodge is not so radical as some later popular writers who erect an antithesis between assent to a proposition and trust in a person; but some paragraphs tend in that direction; and the method he uses is to define truth as trustworthy.

Great philosophic courage is required to say what the primary idea of truth is. Hodge treats the matter too easily. Plato and other ancients tried to define truth as "what is," thus connecting truth with being. No doubt we can trust what is to be. But the primary idea is being. In modern language one might say that trust is "what is so;" or, truth is what is the case. Possibly these definitions are tautological. Maybe truth is indefinable. But in any case it is a misdirected analysis to shift from truth to trust in order to avoid assent.

Not only is the direction wrong, in that it diverges from truth, but the result is frustrating too; for when one drops truth and assent, one must not merely use the word *trust,* one must say what it means. Why should one define truth by trust instead of trust by truth? Why cannot one reverse Hodge's analysis and say that the "primary idea" of trust is assent to the truth? But if a person does not want to admit this, he should define trust. Hodge does not.

Now, strange to say, Hodge concludes the section on page 91 by saying, "What therefore the Scripture means by faith, in this connection, the faith which is required for salvation, is an act of the whole soul, of the understanding, of the heart, and of the will." Precisely! It is an act of the unitary person, in Scripture called the "heart," or the "soul," of whom the activity of understanding and of will are essential, while the feelings and emotions, which Hodge has conveniently omitted here, are irrelevant.

If an evangelist holds to this position he will preach the Gospel. If he has other ideas of faith, he will almost necessarily adulterate the Gospel, alter the message, and handle the Word of God deceitfully.

Chapter Seven

Assurance

Assurance of salvation has some connection with evangelism. Several popular evangelists try to give such assurance to those who come forward. They think a convert should have assurance from the very first moment. In any case the Scripture has a few things to say about assurance, and so the subject is a proper appendix to the previous chapter.

One writer on evangelism proposes a method for developing assurance. Stanley C. Brown in *Evangelism in the Early Church,* previously quoted in chapter three to the effect that Paul never dreamed that people in later ages would be reading his sporadic letters, says that assurance is gained by signing a card, shaking a hand, or some sort of "landmark," accompanied by strong emotion. Then too I listened to an evangelist who came to speak to a group of Christian students on the subject of evangelism. He made quite a point of remembering where you were converted. Fix the picture of the building, the aisle, or the pulpit in mind. Recall how you stood at the front. With such vivid imagery, he told us, you will conquer your doubts. You will have assurance.

This is hardly what the Bible says. No verse directs the convert to sign a card, shake a hand; and certainly no verse promises assurance by means of a vivid visual image of the place at which the conversion took place. The Bible does indeed have something to say about assurance; and if a Christian wants to preach the Gospel and wants to give some human help in developing assurance in his converts, he should proceed according to the Scripture and not according to the unscriptural imaginations of these false prophets.

There are four points that need to be mentioned with respect to assurance. The first point is that assurance is possible. At first sight, this does not seem to contradict the popular evangelists. Assurance is something they emphasize. Yet as the Biblical study continues, it may eventually appear that these evangelists do not really believe in assurance at all. Or, to put it in other words, what they mean by assurance is not what the Bible means. But first, let it be made clear that the Bible teaches assurance.

The Romanists deny assurance. They consider it presumption to claim assurance. The Council of Trent decided that "No one, moreover, so long as he is in this mortal life, ought so far to presume as regards the secret mystery of divine predestination, as to determine for certain that he is assuredly in the number of the predestinate; as if it were true that he that is justified, either cannot sin any more, or, if he do sin, that he ought to promise himself an assured repentance; for except by special revelation, it cannot be known whom God hath chosen unto himself" (Sixth session, Chapter XII).

In our church for many years there was a woman of remarkable gifts. She was no intellectual. She had never gone beyond third grade of grammar school. She married a happy, lovable, somewhat irresponsible carpenter. To increase the small income of those days, she baked bread and collected a small clientele. It was good bread; I know! She was superintendent of our primary department for a long time. No one was more faithful in all the affairs of the church than she. But she had been raised a Roman Catholic, and never entirely got over it. Images and indulgences she left behind. But she always thought that it was presumption to claim assurance of salvation. From all external appearances (and that is all the rest of us could judge by) she was the one who had greatest reason to be assured. But she was not.

Unlike this woman, most people get a sense of assurance much too easily. Everyone who has a smattering of religion, and the smattering may be quite minimal, believes he is going to heaven. A Lutheran girl told me (and surely no Lutheran should have told me this) that she was not perfect but that she was really pretty good, and so she had no reason to think otherwise than that she would get to heaven. Maybe this was not a great degree of assurance, but it was an assurance of sorts.

The people mentioned in Matthew 7:22ff. had assurance. Lord, Lord, have we not prophesied in thy name? But Jesus replied, Depart from me, I never knew you. As the profoundly theological Negro spiritual says, Everybody talkin' 'bout heaven ain't goin' there. Micah 3:11 says, "The heads thereof judge for reward, and the priests thereof teach for hire, and the prophets thereof divine for money yet will they lean upon the Lord and say, Is not the Lord among us? None evil can come upon us."

It is clear therefore that there is a feeling of assurance that is not real assurance. Just because a person believes that he is saved is an insufficient reason for thinking that he is saved. It may be suggested for sober consideration whether or not those who are most easily assured of salvation are least likely to be saved.

Nevertheless, in spite of all hypocrisy and self-deception, it is possible to have assurance. The well-known verse in I John 5:13 says, "These things have I written unto you that believe on the name of the Son of God that ye may know that ye have eternal life." Romans 5:2ff. says, "We . . . rejoice in hope of the glory of God . . . and hope maketh not ashamed." That is to say, our hope shall not be disappointed. We hope to arrive in heaven; and this hope will be satisfied.

This is an assurance that many popular evangelists do not have themselves and cannot promise to their hearers. Yes, they insist on assurance, but it is not the assurance that the Bible teaches. These evangelists, the ones I have in mind, are Arminians. They do not believe in the perseverance of the saints, or, as they call it, eternal security. They claim to be very sure that they are saved now; but they are not sure that they will be saved tomorrow or next week. If they die tonight, they will be in heaven immediately. But if they should live a while longer, they might fall into sin, fall from grace, and then they would be eternally lost. But they are very sure just now. Their mentality is hard to understand. How can anyone be very happy if he thinks he has an eternal life that is so little eternal that it might end next week? How can such a person look to the future with equanimity and confidence if he is so unsure of heaven? Such an evangelist might as well be a Romanist. They talk about being born again, about regeneration; but the kind of regeneration they preach is something that a man must experience as many times as he falls from grace. To be really saved, *i.e.*, to get to heaven, one must be born again over and over again. Their hope therefore is one that can easily disappoint. These preachers often talk quite a lot about the Holy Spirit; but they deny to the Spirit the power to give a man eternal life. By eternal I mean eternal; not a life that ends in the near future. Thus they do not have assurance; nor do they preach the Gospel, for the Gospel promises at least the possibility of assurance. It promises, not the mere possibility of eternal life; it promises eternal life.

This leads to the second point that needs to be mentioned in this chapter. The Gospel promises the possibility of assurance. It does not quite promise every Christian actual assurance. It is strange that some preachers, some evangelists, even those and especially those already described, talk as if one cannot have faith without having assurance. They give the impression that you must know you are saved, if you are saved. But this is not what the Bible says. The verse from I John, quoted just above, said that John wrote the epistle in order that those who read it might be assured. But if regeneration *ipso facto* guaranteed assurance, it would not be necessary to write an epistle encouraging assurance and giving direction on how assurance can be obtained.

Since the epistle was written for this purpose, it is one of the best places in the Bible to find directions. I John 2:3 says, "Hereby we do know that we know him—if we keep his commandments." Recall the lament, "Lord, Lord, have we not prophesied in thy name?" But these people were condemned because they had not acted righteously. They may have walked down the aisle, shaken someone's hand, and signed a card; but they were workers of iniquity. Remembering some emotional experience would do them no good. We know that we know the Lord by keeping his commandments. Another test by which we may come to assurance is given in 3:14, "We know that we have passed from death to life, because we love the brethren." Later in the same chapter it says, "Let us love . . . in deed and in truth; and hereby we know that we are of the truth, and shall assure our hearts before him." Again, "He that keepeth his commandments dwelleth in him, and he in him; and hereby we know that he abideth in us, by the Spirit which he hath given us."

II Peter 1:5 does not explicitly mention assurance, but the section has to do with God's "exceeding great and precious promises" with which he "called us to glory and virtue," so that the remainder of the section describes how we may be assured of profiting by those promises. Verse five then says, "Giving all diligence, add to your faith virtue, and to your virtue knowledge, and to knowledge temperance . . . for if these things be in you, and abound, they shall make you that ye shall be neither barren nor unfruitful in the knowledge of our Lord Jesus Christ."

Without minimizing the other items in this list, it is well to emphasize knowledge. If one wishes assurance, he will try to increase his knowledge. Knowledge is mentioned twice in the section. Therefore, if one wishes assurance that he is regenerated, let him ask himself, Do I study the Scripture? How much of it do I know? Some people know so very little; some people believe so very little; some evangelists must have so very little assurance.

A final note on this point returns us to the Romanists. The Council of Trent said that it would require supernatural revelation to know whether one was predestinated to eternal life. These directions in the Bible on how to attain assurance show that without extraordinary revelation, simply by the right use of the ordinary means, we may attain to the assurance of faith.

A third point concerning assurance is one that is logically implied by what has already been said. Yet it deserves an explicit mention. The Westminster Confession puts the matter very strongly. "This certainty is not a bare conjectural and probable persuasion, grounded upon a fallible hope; but an infallible assurance of faith, founded upon the divine truth of the promises of salvation, the inward evidences of those graces unto which these promises are made, the testimony of the Spirit of adoption witnessing with our spirits that we are the children of God: which Spirit is the earnest of our inheritance, whereby we are sealed to the day of redemption."

Though the wording is very clear, it may be necessary in this age to point out two places where a misunderstanding may arise. First, the infallibility mentioned is not ours, as if we are infallible. The infallibility belongs to the promises of God.

There is no hint here that we rise to the level of the inspired authors of the Bible. This would be a reversal to the Romish position that a supernatural revelation is necessary. All that is necessary is the Scripture. The second point at which a misunderstanding may occur is the reference to the Spirit witnessing with our spirits. Here too, the same idea is involved. The Spirit witnesses *with* our spirits as we study the Bible. He does not witness *to* our spirits, as if giving an additional revelation. Aside from these two matters, the Westminster Confession is clear.

The fourth and last point with reference to assurance is that, although salvation can never be lost, assurance can. That this is so, and that in addition assurance can be restored, is all seen in a very fine passage in Micah 7:7-9: "Therefore I will look unto the Lord; I will wait for the God of my salvation. My God will hear me. Rejoice not against me, O mine enemy; when I fall, I shall arise; when I sit in darkness, the Lord shall be a light unto me. I will bear the indignation of the Lord because I have sinned against him, until he plead my cause and execute judgment for me. He will bring me forth to the light, and I shall behold his righteousness." When David was thus bearing the indignation of the Lord, he prayed, "Restore unto me the joy of thy salvation. . . . Deliver me from bloodguiltiness, O Lord, thou God of my salvation, and my tongue shall sing aloud of thy righteousness."

A Pilgrim's Progress by John Bunyan has a chapter on the loss of assurance. Christian and his new companion Hopeful have recently escaped from the persecutions in Vanity Fair. They recuperate beside still waters and in pleasant pastures. Then it is time to push forward. But the road up from the river is stony, and their feet hurt. So they climb over a stile and proceed along a path that seems to run parallel with the Way. Overtaken by a storm they can neither go forward nor find their way back.

Exhausted, they sleep under some rough shelter. In the morning, Giant Despair, on whose grounds they have been trespassing, finds them, drags them to Doubting Castle, and throws them into his dungeon. He beats them severely, tries to persuade them to commit suicide, and starves them. Finally Christian remembers that he has a key in his pocket that can unlock the doors of the dungeon in the castle. It is the key of promise. With it the two men escape as the Giant falls into one of his occasional fits.

Everybody should have read *A Pilgrim's Progress* when a child—at least a child's version of the story. But also everyone should read it again for the theology. For its theology is not that of Arminian evangelists; it is thorough-going Calvinism.

Chapter Eight
Paradigms of Evangelism

This book opened with some remarks on hillbilly music in an evangelistic campaign, but it has since paid no attention to external methods of evangelism. So far as popular services are concerned (a one-week, two-week, or three-week series of meetings), the only rule that can be given to the evangelist is to prepare a dozen or more sermons that cover a good section of the Biblical message. The apostolic sermons in Acts suggest necessary subjects and indicate a good way of getting started. One must preach the propitiatory sacrifice of Christ to satisfy the justice of his Father. One must preach the Resurrection. These matters entail the doctrine of sin, the federal headship of Adam, justification by faith, and no doubt something on sanctification should be added. Note well that the Apostle Paul did not act on the Canadian evangelist's foolish principle that no one should hear the Gospel twice until everybody has heard it once. Paul stayed months and years in Ephesus and Corinth.

If the so-called Gospel songs, which contain so very little of the Gospel in comparison with *Rock of Ages* and other outstanding hymns, and the silly choruses, and the repulsive dance band music, are all the people can take, I suppose there is no Biblical prohibition against singing just a little of the Gospel if the people refuse to sing more. Furthermore, God will not judge them on their lack of aesthetic sensibility. These higher levels of Christian worship must be left in the hands of the regular pastor who helps his people grow in grace over a period of years. Just be sure that the silly choruses have nothing in them contrary to the Gospel. Some have.

Sermons, evangelistic campaigns, mass meetings—if anyone is able to draw a crowd—make a very easy but relatively ineffective method of evangelization. No, there is nothing wrong in holding large popular meetings. Paul preached in the streets. So have I. But this sort of thing depends for its completion on the audience hearing more of the Gospel at a later date. So Paul taught daily in the synagogue.

If one will read the sermons of Moody, one will be surprised at how little of the Gospel he preached. Billy Sunday is said to have preached an even more restricted message—though I am not sure this was the case. But an evangelist can never preach enough, even a reasonable amount, unless he can continue for six weeks or so.

If there were genuine conversions in the Moody and Sunday meetings, it was because faithful pastors had already explained the Gospel: The evangelists only pressed for a decision. Today so few pastors preach the Gospel, so few people know anything about the Bible, that I doubt the genuineness of the conversion of most of those who come forward to shake the evangelist's hand. Instructional after-meetings are good. But not the fifteen-minute variety. The extent of various individuals' understanding differs, of course, but most people today under- stand almost nothing and require lengthy explanations.

That this is so can better be seen by turning our attention from public services to personal evangelism. In a public service the minister does not know what is in the minds of his auditors. He does not know their objections, their confusions, their ignorance. Those seated in the pews cannot interrupt and ask questions. They can lose the thread of the discourse at the second stitch. But in the conversation of personal work questions and answers reveal something of the auditor's troubles. Even so it is not all smooth sailing.

Dr. Francis Schaeffer in his *The God Who is There,* pages 126-128, gives an excellent example. Those seriously interested should get the book and read it.

Here I shall give a discouraging example of my own. On one occasion I had a half dozen college students coming to our home once a week for six weeks to study Romans. Academically they were good students. One of them was a Roman Catholic. I was very anxious to get this young man to understand justification by faith, by faith alone. Unless he understood what Paul was saying, he could not believe it. Understanding was the first step.

Now I was aware that the Romish idea of justification differs from that of Luther and Calvin. Faith also is differently defined. Grace does not mean the same thing. Merely using these words would have simply confused and misled the student. So I tried very carefully to show that by justification Paul meant a judicial act of acquittal (with acceptance or reconciliation). I went over the text in detail for an hour and a half each night. The students all asked questions.

By the fourth or fifth night I thought the Roman Catholic had come to understand a little bit. But on the sixth evening when I asked him a few simple questions, I was dismayed to see that he had understood virtually nothing at all. So inbred with Catholic ideas was he that he had grasped nothing. I could say my dog had as good an understanding of justification as he had. In fact better, for my dog is not a Romanist.

When some zealous evangelists say how *simple* the Gospel is, I concur that the Gospel is simple in the sense that a great chess move is simple. It is the most effective move in the situation. It combines maximum defense with maximum attack and leads to mate in the fewest possible moves. But a poor chess player does not find it simple or easy. It is like the simplicity of Kepler's three laws of planetary motion over Ptolemy's. Kepler's laws are simpler, but much more difficult to explain. This is not what the popular evangelist means by simple. He thinks the Gospel is easy to understand. Therefore he gives little explanation, little elucidation, little Gospel. Note, however, that Nicodemus, a ruler in Israel, did not easily understand. The early Gentile Christians could hardly understand. Even the Church Fathers were seriously deficient. For three hundred years or more they could not understand the Person of Christ; they learned the Trinity a little faster; but their soteriology, the significance of Christ's death, escaped them for centuries. Justin Martyr, for example, was of course a martyr; he probably was a Christian; but with his view of the Atonement I would not have voted to receive him as a communicant member of our congregation. Recall too that the Apostle Paul anathematized the Judaizers in Galatia, who accepted Christ as Messiah, as their Lord, and who most probably, because of their acquaintance with the Old Testament sacrifices, understood the Atonement far better than Justin did.

Who then can be saved? Fortunately, with God all things are possible, but with us evangelization is usually very difficult. For example, in a certain public school a Christian teacher talked to a Romanist teacher. One of their shorter conversations had to do with a news item in *Time* Magazine. "Well, what do you know about *that!*" said the Roman Catholic teacher. The other queried, "About what?" So the conversation was launched. It seems that modern Roman Catholic theologians have declared that Mary's virginity at the birth of Christ need be only symbolical, not biological, and to the Roman Catholic teacher, that explained everything; why hadn't the Church thought of this before? Wryly, the Christian commented that she hated to see the Roman Catholic Church taking the same road as liberal Protestants had some years ago, and her colleague, not understanding her woeful tone, asked what she meant. Hard put to reducing a century of theological history into one sentence, the Christian replied simply, "Denying the truth of Scripture." The Roman Catholic teacher objected, for the theologians, according to *Time,* had not denied Scripture; they simply said Mary was not really a virgin! When it was pointed out that since Scripture said Mary *was* a virgin, and the theologians said she *wasn't,* they were in fact denying Scripture. Oh, well, maybe so; but, the Romanist wondered, what difference did it make anyway? As long as we understand the symbolism . . . . The difference—and the teacher-evangelist tried to state it as simply as possible—is whether Jesus is the son of Mary and Joseph, and therefore man, or whether he is the son of Mary and the Holy Spirit, and therefore the son of man *and* of God, able to offer the supreme sacrifice to atone for the sins of his people. It is a question of his human and divine natures, and the theologians are emphasizing his humanity to the exclusion of his divinity. A little puzzled, the Roman Catholic looked back at the magazine and then said slowly, "This says they are emphasizing his humanity over his divinity—well! That's just what *you* said! I *never* would have thought of that! How did you figure it out?"

Some examples of evangelism do not commend themselves to a sober mind. In a certain town where I lived for a while a woman met her neighbor on the street. The woman felt compelled to witness, testify, evangelize, or whatever the conversation should be called. She addressed her neighbor somewhat abruptly and said, You are a bad mother to be sending your little girl (age 7) to hell. Just about as abruptly as that. The woman speaking would not send her child to a Christian school, but insisted that her child, also aged 7, should remain in public school. The reason was that if the youngster were in a Christian school, there would be no opportunity to evangelize. The children in the public school needed witnessing and evangelization. Now perhaps the mother thought that her darling did not need the Christian training a Christian school could give, and that her child would not be harmed by the secularism of the public school system; nevertheless the greater number of unbelievers in a school is hardly a good reason for choosing education in one school rather than another.

In contrast with this blunt and brusque form of evangelization, the following is a very different example. Probably it was just as unsuccessful, but at least it was different. The story will be given as a conversation, and many of the sentences will be verbatim. One speaker will be a minister, designated M, a minister who needed to accept the Gospel. The other speaker will be E, the evangelist.

M's first speech here will be a little long and is composed of statements that he made on several different occasions. This seems necessary in order to bring M's state of mind clearly before the reader.

M. I try not to be either Conservative or Liberal. I tell myself that I simply let the Bible speak; I try to read both conservative and liberal publications. I get rather discouraged at times, for both kinds of books waste so much time erecting and destroying to their own satisfaction certain stereotypes, which, however true they may be of unscholarly folk, do not correspond to the liberal and conservative scholars whom I have known.

I do not believe literary analysis of the Pentateuch is the last word in interpretation. However, it does come to my aid when I meet certain problems. Item: The three episodes in Genesis about a man going into a strange land and asking his wife to confess to be his sister, so that his life will not be endangered.

I suppose my main complaint is that I cannot, with the best will in the world—and I have tried!—use the Bible as an external and completely objective proof for God. I don't believe the Sermon on the Mount to have been proved by the miracles of Jesus.

Faith does not come easily to me. The fulcrum of my experience is World War II. It made God a necessity. But, He is not the closed-system God I seem to find among some conservatives, nor the "dear God" of the liberals. The bit I saw of concentration camps made me search at what I believe is a deeper level: and I believe that I have been found there by the God of Jesus, who is not categorized as omnipotent, etc., but who is in His inmost being Love. This basic fact does not require my Bible to be plenarily inspired. And I suppose the reason I react against both conservatives and liberals is that one appears to present a mechanical God tied by His own presuppositions, and the other a mere blob of inchoate good intentions.

I am certain that a part of my problem so far as the so-called Conservative approach to the Bible is concerned is that I (1) do not understand what they are trying to say; (2) do not understand why they think it must be said as they say it.

Let me first state why I am not able to accept the plenary theory of Biblical inspiration. What does plenary inspiration mean? At face value it must mean that the Scriptures as they stand are as they are because God intended them to be that way. When the writers of Scripture wrote, they were immediately in some manner aware of the sentence structure and vocabulary which God intended for His Word to assume. In the Old Testament, they used a Hithpa'el form of the verb, in the New Testament an Aorist Passive, because this is the way God wanted it.

Now, this (if I am at all correct) sounds very much like a "religious" mechanism approach to reality which is at least as suspect as any kind of mechanistic understanding of the nature of things. More than that, I fail to see exactly what, even should it be so, this kind of inspiration means in the face of present evidence. Even if God should have so dictated His Word in the beginning, this is not the way we now possess it. There are differences; and if there are, then I don't quite see the insistence on a perfect original. Am I to assume that God was so very careful with the first copy, and so very careless with the second and third, etc.?

Let me try to state in a sentence what I mean thus far: The doctrine of plenary inspiration seems to me both an *unwarranted* mechanistic theorizing regarding Holy Scripture, and fails to account for the variety in which we now possess that Scripture.

E. At least three times you complain that you are unable to understand what the conservatives, *i.e.,* the historic Protestant position, is trying to say. You also wonder why they are trying to say it. Of course, they are trying to say it because they believe it to be true and important. Why else?

Plenary is an adjective of extent. It refers to the Bible as a whole. Plenary inspiration means that the whole Bible, without exception, is inspired—the geneaologies as much as John 17.

You said that this was "unwarranted theorizing." The warrant is a long list of verses. For example, "All Scripture is given by inspiration of God. . . ." This admits of no exception. Christ said, "The Scripture cannot be broken." He did not choose Psalm 82 because it was more inspired than any other part, but simply because (aside from relevance to the discussion) it was a part of Scripture, and Scripture cannot be broken.

You say that plenary inspiration does not answer the

question it proposes to answer. The question is, I suppose, does all Scripture, some only, or none, come from God? It would seem to me that the answer is unambiguous.

There is another facet of inspiration which you mention in concrete without giving it the usual name. It is the verbal inspiration of Scripture. As *plenary* is an adjective of extent, *verbal* is an adjective of (shall we say) depth. It indicates the manner of inspiration. God "breathed out" the Scriptures in words. Dozens of times, yes, hundreds of times, you have phrases like—I have put my words in thy mouth, the word of the Lord came unto . . . , if ye believe not his writings, how shall ye believe my words? Again, the force of these assertions can be appreciated only after a long list of these expressions has been drawn up.

Conclusion: Plenary and verbal inspiration is the Bible's own explanation of itself.

You seem to say that verbal inspiration is a mechanical affair, and apparently mechanical is a disparaging term. Well, if you mean that verbal inspiration suggests that God acts like a boss dictating a letter to a stenographer, I would reply (1) it is still not disparaging, but (2) this is not what the original Protestants meant. The picture of a stenographer is rather a liberal caricature. The trouble with the picture of a stenographer is not that God controls his writers less than a boss controls his secretary; but God's control is far more extensive. God controls the very thoughts of the writer and the choice of his words. God controls the inner psychology of the prophet, not just his pen.

M. If we truly insist the Bible, literally understood, to be authoritative, why don't we obey it? I'm not talking about the commands which are of such depth in demand. I have in mind, Baptism. Is there any doubt at all that *baptizo* means immersion? Has there ever been any doubt in "historical Protestant scholarship"? Didn't Calvin himself admit immersion to be scriptural? Well. . . . "This is my body," said Jesus. Why do we argue with the Romanists about this, since He said it? And I could go on with other citations. The point I am trying to make is that we deny with our actions what logical consistency causes us to confess with our formal thought.

E. You ask, if the Bible is authoritative, why not obey it? Well, I am all in favor of obeying it. But you say, or you word your sentence so as to cause the inference, that Presbyterians do not obey it because they do not use immersion in baptism. You ask, did not Calvin admit that immersion was Scriptural? I am not sure of this point. I would suppose that he admitted that immersion was satisfactory, since the usual position among us is that the mode makes no difference. Then you ask another question: Is there any doubt at all that baptism *means* immersion? To this I would say that there is considerable doubt. I doubt that it strictly meant immersion (as contrasted with some other form of washing) either in classical Greek words or in New Testament Greek. In Daniel 4:33, *i.e.,* LXX 4:30, one of the Greek words used to say that Nebuchadnezzar was wet with dew is *baptizo.* I can hardly think that this was immersion. Mark 7:4 says that couches were baptized. It seems to me that this means they were washed. In Hebrews 9:10, 13, 19, 21, the several baptisms (King James, washings) were done by sprinkling. In I Corinthians 10:2 the Israelites were baptized, but the Egyptians were immersed. Similarly in I Peter 3:21 Noah was baptized, but the wicked were immersed. It therefore seems rather clear to me that baptism does not mean immerse, and therefore I believe that I obey the Bible, when, as it happened this morning, I baptized the infant daughter of two of our members. But if I should be mistaken, and if I have not obeyed the Bible, such a fact does not undermine the inspiration of the Bible. If it did, you would be requiring a theory that would guarantee me from ever misunderstanding any part of the Bible. You say in your letter that you think you can provide for such a theory, as a substitute for verbal inspiration. Maybe you can; but of one thing I am quite sure: It will not be, as you claim it will be, Biblical.

M. I still am not certain that I understand how you can hold verbal-plenary inspiration. To me, this insistence of yours is meaningless. You admit that this claim applies only to the original manuscripts, which you also say we do not possess. Now, I cannot but conclude from that, that the claim itself is meaningless. Am I incorrect in assuming that the main reason for claiming plenary inspiration (aside from the fact that you believe it to be Biblical, and true) is for its value in vesting the Bible with authority independent of human manipulation? That is what I understand by the insistence on the "objective authority" of the Bible. But, this is vitiated when we admit that we no longer possess this completely authoritative Bible. Whether the errors (possible errors in textual collation) total 44/100% or 99 and 44/100% makes no difference. It is we in our human calculations who decide which alternative reading is acceptable. It is we who decide whether or not this reading affects the whole. More than that, all this ado about original manuscripts appears to make God appear a rather muddled do-gooder, who took infinite care in getting His Word across in the beginning, only to leave its future care to the mercy of every sloppy and sleepy-headed scribe.

E. You say that plenary-verbal inspiration is meaningless. I suppose you really intend to say that it is useless. It can hardly be meaningless. I stated its meaning—simply that God breathed out the words of Scripture, with the obvious result that what the prophets wrote was without error. Is not this meaning clear?

So, I take it you intended to say that this doctrine was useless. Your reason is that even if the scribal errors in the manuscripts are as little as 44/100%, we still have to decide which reading to accept and how it affects the whole. That is, you claim that unless we ourselves are infallible, there is no use in God's speaking the absolute truth. God might as well mix error into his words, for we are going to make mistakes anyway. Now, this does not sound reasonable to me at all. If I ask directions in driving around the country, I may misinterpret the directions; but I would not appreciate my guide's misinforming me, on the ground that I might misunderstand anyhow. A scribe might correctly copy Plato and Aristotle; but it would still be the mistaken views of those men. A scribe might make a few mistakes in copying the Word of God, but we would still have substantially the Word of God. The difference is between a correct copy of error and a slightly incorrect copy of truth. I cannot agree that the latter is useless.

M. I begin with a question, the basic question. Is there a God? If there is, can I know Him? My answer to this question, If there is a God, I cannot know it unless He tells me about Himself. I can study His doing, Nature; but what shall my conclusion about God be? That He is kind and benevolent? Or that Nature is vicious and careless? I think it is obvious that whatever I see in Nature, and whichever I emphasize, will be for reasons of personal experience and inclination. This makes an incarnational religion imperative, and this is precisely what we have in Jesus Christ. You will ask, Which Jesus Christ? and I will answer, the One to whom the New Testament Scriptures witness.

My Bible does not have to be absolute. It must be sufficiently so that it compels me to face the Absolute, the One who speaks through His Son, and points backward and forward from that crucial Son. This is precisely what I find in the Bible.

E. You raise first the question of God's existence. You give reasons that it could be only by revelation that a knowledge of God would be possible. I quite agree with this so far. And in particular I agree with what I take to be your inference that the cosmological argument is invalid.

However, your next sentence is: "This makes an incarnational religion imperative." How so? This is an inference that I can by no means follow.

The fact that if we are to know God at all it must be by a self-revelation no more implies one than another of the following statements; We do not know God at all; God reveals Himself to us in intuitions or in mystic trances and not in incarnation; God reveals Himself to us in intelligible and true propositions; and finally, it remains possible that there is no God at all. Now, I fail to see how you come to accept the position that there must be an incarnation. These other possibilities still remain. You have given no reason that rules them out.

Only after you have made this great leap do you speak of the New Testament as a witness to the incarnate Christ. But we cannot have the least idea of even the possibility of an incarnation until after we accept the Scripture. And second, if the New Testament is completely wrong when it claims that it consists of the words of God, why should we believe its supposed witness to Christ? All we know of Christ comes from the Scripture.

M. I take it you would agree with me that my view of the Bible is not self-sustaining, but it is a part of my total view of reality. That is, I don't come to the Bible as a *tabula rasa* mind. Neither is it my total experience, but one among many. It forms a part (and informs a part) of my reality, but not all of it.

I do not believe something just because "It's in the Bible." Something is not true, just because "the Bible says." It cannot contradict my total experience of reality, or else I would not accept it.

What I am leading up to is simply this: By a complicated combination of experience, trial and error, idea and accident, I come to a something that is signified by the word "reality." If I am not reflective, it will be rather inchoate; if I am reflective, it should have some coherence. The Bible is a part of this, and as I read it, listen to its claims, follow its implications, I do so in so far as it finds a harmony with my total view of reality. It tells me there is a God. Yes. Reality doesn't seem to be complete in itself. It appears dependent. It tells me God revealed Himself. Yes, if there is a God, He would have to do this, if we are to know Him. It tells me of a Resurrection from the Dead. This is not so easily set into reality. Yet, how else am I to account for the obvious historical phenomena of a Church which apparently has always believed and taught this, which has suffered and died for this faith, which has evidenced the power of renewal which a living Lord would bring?

I read also of a Creation in seven (apparently) 24-hour days. This is of still another order. I can find no place for it in my total view; for I am committed (logically, emotionally, experientially) to another understanding, which speaks in terms of process, of millions of years, and which is an outgrowth of a still larger discipline of understanding in terms of procedure and experience. What am I to do? I cannot call the first account simply foolishness, for it is part and parcel of the total view. Well, I read it again. What is it claiming? That it presents an observed and verified account of what actually happened? It is possible to understand it another way: It tells me that the cosmos is dependent, that whatever this great process is that I experience and study, it is not self-existent. Aha. This fits with all the rest again.

I keep on reading the Bible. Some of its parts I do not understand. Other parts I understand and do not accept. But, I do accept them in the biblical sense, not in the literal sense.

Some of the miracles attributed to Jesus are difficult to fit into my total view of reality in question; but I don't have enough information. For example, casting out the demons into the swine, and their running into the sea. I don't think we have enough information to decide if this is "exactly" what happened, and only what happened.

Now, what right have I to pick and choose? After all, the Bible claims that all of it is inspired, is authoritative, and so on. Who am I to set myself up as judge and jury? But, we cannot help doing this, and this is what we are always doing. We cannot help doing it, for it is "I" who decide, in any case.

This is the basis of my "selecting" as you call it. I do not need a verbally inspired Bible. I do need one that is accurate enough to fulfill its purpose: namely, the testimony to God who was in Christ. The Bible is certainly accurate enough for this, as millions of lives testify.

E. You begin with the theme that a theory of inspiration is a part of one's total world-view; one's use of the Bible is part of one's response to the totality of reality. With this I am in complete agreement, if we use the words in the same sense. No one more than I insists on the necessity of a single self-consistent world-view. Therefore I would also agree with you that the Bible cannot contradict my total experience of reality. Your words are, "cannot contradict my total experience of reality." But while I am willing to make this assertion, I am not sure that you can properly do so. It would seem from several things you say that there are a number of statements in the Bible that contradict your world-view. In fact, you immediately suggest that you would not accept this or that if it contradicted your total experience. Hence, in answer to my question in my last letter, How do you decide to accept some of the Bible's statements and reject others? you answer that you test the Bible by your experience; you do not accept something as true, just because the Bible says it. But you develop a criterion from experience and measure the Bible by that criterion.

In your total experience you are reading the Bible. You say, "It tells me there is a God. . . . It tells me God revealed himself. . . . It tells me of a Resurrection." But if you do not accept the truth of propositions on the basis of the Bible's assertion, you cannot accept these points without confirmation from experience. Now, I am willing to go to bat for hours against the view that experience can show us the existence of God. The alleged proofs are all fallacies. But there is nothing in experience to substantiate your statement, "if there is a God, he would have to reveal himself." Of course, he would have to reveal himself *if* we are to know him. But the existence of God does not imply that God wishes man to know him.

Now if one accepts a statement as true simply because the Bible says so, historical events like the crucifixion and the Resurrection are automatically accepted. But this is not the way you do things. However, I wish to make a further point. The acceptance of these historical events is not nearly enough to constitute Christianity. Several people have risen from the dead —at least the Bible says so. The peculiar importance of Christ's Resurrection depends on the interpretation given to the event. Similarly, many people have been crucified, but Christ's crucifixion is not in the same class with the others because of the explanation of the event. Christ died—for our sins, and this latter phrase sums up the whole scriptural doctrine: Christ died for our sins according to the Scriptures; and he rose again for our justification. Now, if you accept the events as you would the events of Caesar's Gallic wars, there remains the question, how does your world-view incline you to accept or reject the specific interpretations of these events that the Bible gives?

You say of a certain view, "Aha, this fits with all the rest." But you have not given me enough of all the rest to see how anything fits. After all I cannot guess why one hesitates at the devils being cast into the swine, if one accepts the Resurrection. You say you do not have enough information about the swine incident to make a decision. Have you enough information about the Resurrection? The only information about both is that the Bible says so.

Your insistence that a person must make a decision is beside the point. Of course it is you and I who decide. But the point at issue is, On what grounds do you and I decide? I want to know your reason for accepting a resurrection and rejecting the swine episode.

The conclusion that you draw is in my opinion quite untrue. You say, "all of us choose among the Scriptures, emphasizing some, darkening others." I suppose your literary fluency led you to say *darkening* instead of rejecting; but I suppose also that you mean rejecting, for that is the theme of the argument. But it is untrue that everybody accepts some and rejects other parts of the Bible. I do not; and, not to rile you, J.Y. does not. And I am trying to make the point that you must, if you wish to hold a consistent system, state the grounds, the reasons, for accepting part and rejecting part; and not merely say you and I must decide.

But if there is a revelation, there can be no criterion for it. God cannot swear by a greater; therefore he has sworn by himself. One cannot ask one's own experience to judge God and determine whether God tells the truth or not. Consider Abraham. How could Abraham be sure that God commanded him to sacrifice Isaac? Maybe this suggestion was of the devil; maybe it was a queer auto-suggestion. There is no higher answer to this question than God himself. The final criterion is merely God's statement. It cannot be tested by any superior truth.

At this point the discussion will be broken off, though in real life it continued a long time further. Two remarks should be made. The minister, who thought he was so conservative, consistently denied that Jesus was Lord. He did this by refusing to accept what Jesus said. He refused to accept Jesus' view of the Old Testament and he refused to accept some of Jesus' statements in the New. To acknowledge Jesus as Lord one must accept Jesus' teaching on whatever subject Jesus speaks. The second remark has to do with the evangelist's conduct of the discussion. Some who think themselves to be evangelistic assert that the evangelist must press the matter of sin. Insist that the prospect is a sinner. Make him face his sin. Do not wander off on theological discussions. In reply to this objection one must first note that it is a sin to deny what Jesus said. If Jesus places his stamp of approval on the Old Testament and says that the Scripture cannot be broken, then it is a sin to pick and choose. In the second place, the advice to avoid "wandering" off on theological discussions is also the sin of refusing to accept Jesus' Lordship. When Jesus met the woman at the well, it is true that he spoke to her about her sin of having had many husbands. But it would seem that he did this more to make her recognize that he was a "prophet" than to whack her over the head with her sin, sin, sin. In any case, she asked him a theological question: Does God want us to worship in Jerusalem or here in this mountain? Far from telling the woman to forget her question and keep her mind on the man she now had who was not her husband, Jesus answered her question. He told her that the Jews were right and that the Samaritans were wrong. Jerusalem to that present time was the place of God's choice. But, Jesus continued, in a very short time the place will make no difference because God is about to initiate a new administration of the covenant of grace, and the important thing will be to worship God in spirit and in truth. Note too that this discourse on acceptable worship was not given to Nicodemus, but to the sinful woman at the well.

The woman at the well accepted Jesus as Messiah and Lord. The minister above stedfastly refused.

Let it not be thought that we should not press home the fact of sin. The point is that other matters are also to be brought to light.

During the Billy Sunday campaigns one of his helpers, Fred Seibert, published a little booklet, *Rescue the Perishing,* of 130 pages, three inches by not quite six, with the sub-title, *Personal Work Made Easy—Suggestions for Beginners.* Under a list of headings, Confession, Christ, Christian Science, Conversions, Doubter, Excuses, down to Unpardonable Sin, Worldly Amusements, and Young Converts, the author had collected series of Scripture verses plus a few short paragraphs of advice. In some ways this little booklet was very helpful. It brought to one's attention a long list of verses and how to use them. Without such a list a "beginner" might have trouble remembering them—even if he knew them—and applying them with proper relevance. For example, under "Excuses" there is one page devoted to verses by which to answer the claim "I am not good enough to be a Christian." The next page is headed, "I am too great a sinner." Unfortunately I have found few people who use this excuse. Many more are described under the two preceding pages, "I am good enough," and "I am not very bad." The verses given by Mr. Seibert are relevant enough; but what if the person replies, Of course that is what the Bible says, but I do not believe that the Bible is true?

This is the reason why it is unscriptural to press the question of sin and avoid so-called theological hairsplitting. Sin is a theological concept. It is not just wrong-doing in some ordinary sense. Many people, most people, possibly all people will admit that they have done some wrong. This does not entail their admission that they have sinned. Sin is transgression of the law of God. Or, more fully, sin is any want of conformity unto or transgression of the law of God. To be convicted of sin, one must believe in God, must believe that God has given a law, that God has given the laws in the Bible, and that breaking these laws is an offense against God, deserving of God's wrath and curse. Without this theological foundation the evangelist cannot successfully show that a man is a sinner. When a man says that he does not believe in God, or that he does not believe the Bible is God's word, or that God did not give the laws in the Bible, or that these laws do not apply today, the evangelist has a large task ahead of him before the man can be shown that he stands in need of salvation from the wrath of God.

The following are the words, almost verbatim, of one person who more or less fits the above description.

"There are 356 different religious groups in this country. Each is sure it knows the will of God and each disagrees with every other, on important matters. Most of the groups, all of which claim to be monotheistic, are not. They profess to believe in Jehovah or the Trinity, but a surprising lot of them also believe in a second God, whom they call the devil. True, they do not worship him, but a belief in his existence belies their alleged monotheism."

It is not my intention here to comment on the views of this person, or to correct his misunderstandings. The aim is simply to report his words and show the type of mind with which an evangelist has to deal.

"An enormous amount of good among men has been done in the name of Christ, but when I think of the pain and suffering which have been inflicted and the blood which has been shed in his name by those who were absolutely certain they knew God's will and were imposing it on others, I wonder whether or not the total good exceeds the total harm.

"Moses imposed capital punishment for serious crimes. Does this justify capital punishment today? What choice did Moses have? He was on the move for forty years and did not have an opportunity to build jails. Further, Do we revere liars and cheats if they are successful? Or do we punish them? Jacob got away with the theft of Esau's patrimony and is revered in the Old Testament. What about incest? Lot slept with his two daughters. True, it was more their fault than his, but the incest is not condemned. David. . . . Solomon. . . . If a married woman rather than a married man committed adultery, she was stoned to death. All this is sufficient for me to have a horror of any attempt to base our present laws on the Old Testament, and even more horror at the thought of some religious group putting its own construction of ambiguous parts of the Bible into present day law."

So much for this one person, who in addition had some other things to say. The state of mind is widespread. It is the result of the American public school system, at least to a large measure. For example, as a camouflage for the Supreme Court's attempt to suppress all Christian teaching in the schools, some people have called for a study of the Bible as literature. This is supposed to get a little Christianity into the atheistic schools. In one high school the course in Bible was given to an accommodating teacher who had no strong ideas one way or the other. She wanted to teach the course from a strictly neutral point of view and avoid all controversy. She assigned a paper to be written. One pupil asked if he might write on Isaiah. She asked in return, Do you want to write on First Isaiah or Second Isaiah? The point is obvious. She thought that there was no controversy over the fact that the book of Isaiah was written by one man, Isaiah. She had never heard that there was only one Isaiah. She had been taught when she was a pupil that there are two Isaiahs. And so she "neutrally" taught this "non-controversial" view to her pupils.

Because of certain arrangements I happen to hear a professor teaching the Old Testament to a class. The class meets three times a week, and I have overheard what he is saying a dozen times or so. He constantly and calmly describes the uncivilized superstitions of the Old Testament. He shows all the contradictions between the E account of creation in Genesis 1 and the J account in Genesis 2. Moses (who did not write the Pentateuch) lived in a barbarous age. He enforced a system of sacrifices. Later on the Prophets invented a better religion and taught that God does not require sacrifice. And so on. This professor's students hear nothing from the Biblical viewpoint. The plainest statements are garbled and distorted. As one of his students confidently stated, "I cannot imagine that the writer of Genesis really thought that Adam was a particular individual." But what else could the student say, when he had heard nothing else? What then must an evangelist do when he speaks to such students? They do not believe the Bible. They do not think of God as the Bible presents him. They despise the Mosaic laws, the precepts of Proverbs, and all "rules" of action. To obey divine laws is "legalism" and our only guide of conduct should be love. If we love our neighbor's wife, it is right and good to commit adultery with her. Let us have no laws. Just love.

Should the evangelist tell them to accept Christ? Well, they already accept Christ. Wasn't he the man who stressed love? Of course he was not virgin born. But he died a martyr to his convictions. Why, Christ is more to be honored than even Gandhi. Of course we believe in Christ. We have a personal attachment to him. He opposed the establishment. So too we must demonstrate against the government and tear it down. We are real Christians, relevant to our day. . . . I wonder what Moody could have done with these students.

He could have quoted Scripture verses. Now, it is not such a bad idea to quote Scripture verses. Of course a preacher, an evangelist, a personal worker is not supposed to do nothing but quote. He is also supposed to explain. And one of the most important tasks of the evangelist, an absolutely essential task, is to explain what Christianity is. American education almost guarantees that young people shall have no knowledge of the Bible. They are equally unfamiliar with the claims of Christ and the particulars of the Ten Commandments. Many of my own students have never seen the inside of a Bible. Quote them something and they will assign it to Shakespeare, rather than to David for example. Since they have no idea of what sin is, they have no idea of what salvation is. If they have read Dante, they know that Judas was an associate of Brutus. From their Shakespeare class they have learned that Brutus was the noblest Roman of them all. So probably Judas was some ancient philanthropist who murdered a tyrant. But then again they may know less about Shakespeare and Dante than about the Bible, for everybody knows that the Bible is full of myths.

Now, the Bible makes it quite plain that God is omnipotent and that his grace is irresistible. It is a good thing too, for otherwise no one would repent. God can convert the most unlikely prospects. He converted Saul. So none of these students is beyond hope. Nevertheless, there is a verse about casting pearls before swine; and at times it may be wise not to be too optimistic about the probable results. Here is one final example.

After lunch a group of college students was sitting in the student lounge, waiting a few minutes before going into the chess room to play chess. There were eight or ten in the group. An elderly gentleman sat down with them. This happened in the twenties and the gentleman was a free thinker of the nineteenth century stamp. Not many of them remained, even at that date.

He discoursed on the beauty of Democritus and the philosophy of mechanism. Christianity was all superstition. In fact the Bible says . . . and in trying to reproduce Matthew he made a few simple factual blunders. One of the students had a New Testament in his pocket and a rapid series of thoughts in his mind. Should he correct the old gentleman's account and then try to answer the objection that the man really meant? Then the student remembered the great wisdom of P.T. Barnum, "Never give a sucker an even break." So feigning ignorance and stupidity, which was easy enough for a college junior to do, he asked with a look of amazement, "Is that what the Bible says?" "It certainly does," replied the old man, and he continued by repeating Matthew with even worse mistakes. The student took out his Testament and, handing it to the man, said, Please show it to me. The gentleman picked up the Testament in some confusion, turned a half a dozen pages, slammed the little book down on the table, got up, and walked off.

The student had not preached the Gospel to the free thinker, but he may have made a slight impression on the other students.

These examples, perhaps wrongly labeled paradigms of evangelism, describe pretty well the minds of those to whom the Gospel must be preached today. These people will not be saved directly by lessons in archaeology or by having their Biblical criticism corrected or by refutations of existentialism. But unless the evangelist can talk intelligently on these subjects, he will quickly lose his audience. He may lose it anyway, as Paul did on Mars Hill, but at least he must begin at the point at which his auditors stand. They "know" that religious language is symbolic, that God, if there be a God, could not express his thought in fallible English or Greek. The "Easter Event," graciously left undefined, is a valuable symbol of optimism and courage; but one should not seek truth in value. Undoubtedly

God speaks in history; only he does not say anything.

To such people Christianity must be preached. The evangelist must gain their attention. With a little criticism or existentialism as bait, he can try to insert into the conversation the definition of sin. It will be a new idea to these people. The concept of sin presupposes the concept of law. This must be made clear. Justification must be explained. It is a legal term. Should religion be based on legality? Well, should it be based on illegality? After this is chewed over a little, the idea of a propitiatory sacrifice must be elucidated. It will require a good bit of elucidation. Questions of penology will arise. Penology reminds one of capital punishment and Moses. Some attention must be paid to the Mosaic authorship of the Pentateuch. Fortunately the Dead Sea Scrolls will help with "second" Isaiah. To ignore this, as some so-called evangelists do, will simply strengthen the paganism of the auditor and convince him all the more that Christians are stupid and that Christianity is superstition. If an evangelist is concerned for the soul of his auditor, he must do his best to prevent this result.

By keeping the conversation going, it will be possible to present some of the Christian message. Find some point the student is interested in and explain it carefully. The aim is to *teach*. Christ said, "Teaching them . . . all things." Teach patiently, calmly, and in great detail. This will require the evangelist to diverge from the initial point of interest and explain how this point implies something else. The aim is to teach the *system of doctrine* that the Scriptures teach. The Scriptures are not a haphazard collection of bits of information and theory. They present an integrated, logical system. Justification (carefully explained) produces sanctification (carefully explained). The forgiveness of sin requires a propitiatory sacrifice. The Lordship of Christ implies the Mosaic authorship of the Pentateuch. The Gospel cannot be true unless Christ rose from the dead.

It is impossible to teach the system of doctrine in five minutes, or to reduce it to five spiritual laws, recently discovered by psychology. The Christian message is the whole Bible; it is the whole counsel of God. All of it must be taught, not just a small part, for it is *all* profitable for doctrine, for reproof, for correction, for instruction in righteousness. It is by taking heed thereto that a young man may cleanse his way.

Evangelism is the exposition of the Scripture. God will do the regenerating.

Index

Scripture Index

The Crisis of Our Time

Historians have christened the thirteenth century the Age of Faith and termed the eighteenth century the Age of Reason. The twentieth century has been called many things: the Atomic Age, the Age of Inflation, the Age of the Tyrant, the Age of Aquarius. But it deserves one name more than the others: the Age of Irrationalism. Contemporary secular intellectuals are anti-intellectual. Contemporary philosophers are anti-philosophy. Contemporary theologians are anti-theology.

In past centuries secular philosophers have generally believed that knowledge is possible to man. Consequently they expended a great deal of thought and effort trying to justify knowledge. In the twentieth century, however, the optimism of the secular philosophers has all but disappeared. They despair of knowledge.

Like their secular counterparts, the great theologians and doctors of the church taught that knowledge is possible to man. Yet the theologians of the twentieth century have repudiated that belief. They also despair of knowledge. This radical skepticism has filtered down from the philosophers and theologians and penetrated our entire culture, from television to music to literature. *The Christian in the twentieth century is confronted with an overwhelming cultural consensus—sometimes stated explicitly, but most often implicitly: Man does not and cannot know anything truly.*

What does this have to do with Christianity? Simply this: If man can know nothing truly, man can truly know nothing. We cannot know that the Bible is the Word of God, that Christ died for sin, or that Christ is alive today at the right hand of the Father. Unless knowledge is possible, Christianity is nonsensical, for it claims to be knowledge. What is at stake in the twentieth century is not simply a single doctrine, such as the Virgin Birth, or the existence of hell, as important as those doctrines may be, but the whole of Christianity itself. If knowledge is not possible to man, it is worse than silly to argue points of doctrine—it is insane.

The irrationalism of the present age is so thorough-going and pervasive that even the Remnant—the segment of the professing church that remains faithful—has accepted much of it, frequently without even being aware of what it was accepting. In some circles this irrationalism has become synonymous with piety and humility, and those who oppose it are denounced as rationalists—as though to be logical were a sin. Our contemporary anti-theologians make a contradiction and call it a Mystery. The faithful ask for truth and are given Paradox. If any balk at swallowing the absurdities of the anti-theologians, they are frequently marked as heretics or schismatics who seek to act independently of God.

There is no greater threat facing the true Church of Christ at this moment than the irrationalism that now controls our entire culture. Communism, guilty of tens of millions of murders, including those of millions of Christians, is to be feared, but not nearly so much as the idea that we do not and cannot know the truth. Hedonism, the popular philosophy of America, is not to be feared so much as the belief that logic —that "mere human logic," to use the religious irrationalists' own phrase—is futile. The attacks on truth, on revelation, on the intellect, and on logic are renewed daily. But note well: The misologists—the haters of logic—use logic to demonstrate the futility of using logic. The anti-intellectuals construct intricate intellectual arguments to prove the insufficiency of the intellect. The anti-theologians use the revealed Word of God to show that there can be no revealed Word of God—or that if there could, it would remain impenetrable darkness and Mystery to our finite minds.

Nonsense Has Come

Is it any wonder that the world is grasping at straws—the straws of experientialism, mysticism and drugs? After all, if people are told that the Bible contains insoluble mysteries, then is not a flight into mysticism to be expected? On what grounds can it be condemned? Certainly not on logical grounds or Biblical grounds, if logic is futile and the Bible unintelligible. Moreover, if it cannot be condemned on logical or Biblical grounds, it cannot be condemned at all. If people are going to have a religion of the mysterious, they will not adopt Christianity: They will have a genuine mystery religion. "Those who call for Nonsense," C.S. Lewis once wrote, "will find that it comes." And that is precisely what has happened. The popularity of Eastern mysticism, of drugs, and of religious experience is the logical consequence of the irrationalism of the twentieth century. There can and will be no Christian revival—and no reconstruction of society—unless and until the irrationalism of the age is totally repudiated by Christians.

The Church Defenseless

Yet how shall they do it? The spokesmen for Christianity

have been fatally infected with irrationalism. The seminaries, which annually train thousands of men to teach millions of Christians, are the finishing schools of irrationalism, completing the job begun by the government schools and colleges. Some of the pulpits of the most conservative churches (we are not speaking of the apostate churches) are occupied by graduates of the anti-theological schools. These products of modern anti-theological education, when asked to give a reason for the hope that is in them, can generally respond with only the intellectual analogue of a shrug—a mumble about Mystery. They have not grasped—and therefore cannot teach those for whom they are responsible—the first truth: "And ye shall know the truth." Many, in fact, explicitly deny it, saying that, at best, we possess only "pointers" to the truth, or something "similar" to the truth, a mere analogy. Is the impotence of the Christian Church a puzzle? Is the fascination with pentecostalism and faith healing among members of conservative churches an enigma? Not when one understands the sort of studied nonsense that is purveyed in the name of God in the seminaries.

The Trinity Foundation

The creators of The Trinity Foundation firmly believe that theology is too important to be left to the licensed theologians —the graduates of the schools of theology. They have created The Trinity Foundation for the express purpose of teaching the faithful all that the Scriptures contain—not warmed over, baptized, secular philosophies. Each member of the board of directors of The Trinity Foundation has signed this oath: "I believe that the Bible alone and the Bible in its entirety is the Word of God and, therefore, inerrant in the autographs. I believe that the system of truth presented in the Bible is best summarized in the Westminster Confession of Faith. So help me God."

The ministry of The Trinity Foundation is the presentation of the system of truth taught in Scripture as clearly and as completely as possible. We do not regard obscurity as a virtue, nor confusion as a sign of spirituality. Confusion, like all error, is sin, and teaching that confusion is all that Christians can hope for is doubly sin.

The presentation of the truth of Scripture necessarily involves the rejection of error. The Foundation has exposed and will continue to expose the irrationalism of the twentieth century, whether its current spokesman be an existentialist philosopher or a professed Reformed theologian. We oppose anti-intellectualism, whether it be espoused by a neo-orthodox theologian or a fundamentalist evangelist. We reject misology, whether it be on the lips of a neo-evangelical or those of a Roman Catholic charismatic. To each error we bring the brilliant light of Scripture, proving all things, and holding fast to that which is true.

The Primacy of Theory

The ministry of The Trinity Foundation is not a "practical" ministry. If you are a pastor, we will not enlighten you on how to organize an ecumenical prayer meeting in your community or how to double church attendance in a year. If you are a homemaker, you will have to read elsewhere to find out how to become a total woman. If you are a businessman, we will not tell you how to develop a social conscience. The professing church is drowning in such "practical" advice.

The Trinity Foundation is unapologetically theoretical in its outlook, believing that theory without practice is dead, and that practice without theory is blind. The trouble with the professing church is not primarily in its practice, but in its theory. Christians do not know, and many do not even care to know, the doctrines of Scripture. Doctrine is intellectual, and Christians are generally anti-intellectual. Doctrine is ivory tower philosophy, and they scorn ivory towers. The ivory tower, however, is the control tower of a civilization. It is a fundamental, theoretical·mistake of the practical men to think that they can be merely practical, for practice is always the practice of some theory. The relationship between theory and practice is the relationship between cause and effect. If a person believes correct theory, his practice will tend to be correct. The practice of contemporary Christians is immoral because it is the practice of false theories. It is a major theoretical mistake of the practical men to think that they can ignore the ivory towers of the philosophers and theologians as irrelevant to their lives. Every action that the "practical" men take is governed by the thinking that has occurred in some ivory tower—whether that tower be the British Museum, the Academy, a home in Basel, Switzerland, or a tent in Israel.

In Understanding Be Men

It is the first duty of the Christian to understand correct theory—correct doctrine—and thereby implement correct practice. This order—first theory, then practice—is both logical and Biblical. It is, for example, exhibited in Paul's epistle to the Romans, in which he spends the first eleven chapters expounding theory and the last five discussing practice. The contemporary teachers of Christians have not only reversed the order, they have inverted the Pauline emphasis on theory and practice. The virtually complete failure of the teachers of the professing church to instruct the faithful in correct doctrine is the cause of the misconduct and cultural impotence of Christians. The

Church's lack of power is the result of its lack of truth. The *Gospel* is the power of God, not religious experience or personal relationship. The Church has no power because it has abandoned the Gospel, the good news, for a religion of experientialism. Twentieth century American Christians are children carried about by every wind of doctrine, not knowing what they believe, or even if they believe anything for certain.

The chief purpose of The Trinity Foundation is to counteract the irrationalism of the age and to expose the errors of the teachers of the church. Our emphasis—on the Bible as the sole source of truth, on the primacy of the intellect, on the supreme importance of correct doctrine, and on the necessity for systematic and logical thinking—is almost unique in Christendom. To the extent that the church survives—and she will survive and flourish—it will be because of her increasing acceptance of these basic ideas and their logical implications.

We believe that the Trinity Foundation is filling a vacuum in Christendom. We are saying that Christianity is intellectually defensible—that, in fact, it is the only intellectually defensible system of thought. We are saying that God has made the wisdom of this world—whether that wisdom be called science, religion, philosophy, or common sense—foolishness. We are appealing to all Christians who have not conceded defeat in the intellectual battle with the world to join us in our efforts to raise a standard to which all men of sound mind can repair.

The love of truth, of God's Word, has all but disappeared in our time. We are committed to and pray for a great instauration. But though we may not see this reformation of Christendom in our lifetimes, we believe it is our duty to present the whole counsel of God because Christ has commanded it. The results of our teaching are in God's hands, not ours. Whatever those results, His Word is never taught in vain, but always accomplishes the result that He intended it to accomplish. Professor

Gordon H. Clark has stated our view well:

> There have been times in the history of God's people, for example, in the days of Jeremiah, when refreshing grace and widespread revival were not to be expected: the time was one of chastisement. If this twentieth century is of a similar nature, individual Christians here and there can find comfort and strength in a study of God's Word. But if God has decreed happier days for us and if we may expect a world-shaking and genuine spiritual awakening, then it is the author's belief that a zeal for souls, however necessary, is not the sufficient condition. Have there not been devout saints in every age, numerous enough to carry on a revival? Twelve such persons are plenty. What distinguishes the arid ages from the period of the Reformation, when nations were moved as they had not been since Paul preached in Ephesus, Corinth, and Rome, is the latter's fullness of knowledge of God's Word. To echo an early Reformation thought, when the ploughman and the garage attendant know the Bible as well as the theologian does, and know it better than some contemporary theologians, then the desired awakening shall have already occurred.

In addition to publishing books, of which *Today's Evangelism: Counterfeit or Genuine?* is the twenty-eighth, the Foundation publishes a bimonthly newsletter, *The Trinity Review*. Subscriptions to *The Review* are free; please write to the address below to become a subscriber. If you would like further information or would like to join us in our work, please let us know.

The Trinity Foundation is a non-profit foundation tax-exempt under section 501 (c)(3) of the Internal Revenue Code of 1954. You can help us disseminate the Word of God through your tax-deductible contributions to the Foundation.

And we know that the Son of God is come, and hath given us an understanding, that we may know him that is true, and we are in him that is true, in his Son Jesus Christ. This is the true God, and eternal life.

John W. Robbins
President

Intellectual Ammunition

The Trinity Foundation is committed to the reconstruction of philosophy and theology along Biblical lines. We regard God's command to bring all our thoughts into conformity with Christ very seriously, and the books listed below are designed to accomplish that goal. They are written with two subordinate purposes: (1) to demolish all secular claims to knowledge; and (2) to build a system of truth based upon the Bible alone.

Works of Philosophy

Behaviorism and Christianity, Gordon H. Clark $5.95
     Behaviorism *is a critique of both secular and religious behaviorists. It includes chapters on John Watson, Edgar S. Singer Jr., Gilbert Ryle, B.F. Skinner, and Donald MacKay. Clark's refutation of behaviorism and his argument for a Christian doctrine of man are unanswerable.*

A Christian Philosophy of Education, Gordon H. Clark $8.95
     The first edition of this book was published in 1946. It sparked the contemporary interest in Christian schools. Dr. Clark has thoroughly revised and updated it, and it is needed now more than ever. Its chapters include: The Need for a World-View, The Christian World-View, The

Alternative to Christian Theism, Neutrality, Ethics, The Christian Philosophy of Education, Academic Matters, Kindergarten to University. Three appendices are included as well: The Relationship of Public Education to Christianity, A Protestant World-View, and Art and the Gospel.

A Christian View of Men and Things, Gordon H. Clark $9.95
    No other book achieves what A Christian View *does: the presentation of Christianity as it applies to history, politics, ethics, science, religion, and epistemology. Clark's command of both worldly philosophy and Scripture is evident on every page, and the result is a breathtaking and invigorating challenge to the wisdom of this world.*

Clark Speaks From The Grave, Gordon H. Clark $3.95
    Dr. Clark chides some of his critics for their failure to defend Christianity competently. Clark Speaks *is a stimulating and illuminating discussion of the errors of contemporary apologists.*

Education, Christianity, and the State $7.95
J. Gresham Machen
    Machen was one of the foremost educators, theologians, and defenders of Christianity in the twentieth century. The author of numerous scholarly books, Machen saw clearly that if Christianity is to survive and flourish, a system of Christian grade schools must be established. This collection of essays captures his thought on education over nearly three decades.

Gordon H. Clark: Personal Recollections, $6.95
John W. Robbins, editor
    Friends of Dr. Clark have written their recollections of the man. Contributors include family members, colleagues, students, and friends such as Harold Lindsell, Carl Henry, Ronald Nash, Dwight Zeller, and Mary Crumpacker. The book includes an extensive bibliography of Clark's work.

John Dewey, Gordon H. Clark $2.00
America has not produced many philosophers, but John Dewey has been extremely influential. Clark examines his philosophy of Instrumentalism.

Logic, Gordon H. Clark $8.95
Written as a textbook for Christian schools, Logic *is another unique book from Clark's pen. His presentation of the laws of thought, which must be followed if Scripture is to be understood correctly, and which are found in Scripture itself, is both clear and thorough.* Logic *is an indispensable book for the thinking Christian.*

The Philosophy of Science and Belief in God $5.95
Gordon H. Clark
In opposing the contemporary idolatry of science, Clark analyzes three major aspects of science: the problem of motion, Newtonian science, and modern theories of physics. His conclusion is that science, while it may be useful, is always false; and he demonstrates its falsity in numerous ways. Since science is always false, it can offer no objection to the Bible and Christianity.

Religion, Reason and Revelation, Gordon H. Clark $7.95
One of Clark's apologetical masterpieces, Religion, Reason and Revelation *has been praised for the clarity of its thought and language. It includes chapters on Is Christianity a Religion? Faith and Reason, Inspiration and Language, Revelation and Morality, and God and Evil. It is must reading for all serious Christians.*

Thales to Dewey: A History of Philosophy, paper $11.95
Gordon H. Clark hardback $16.95
This volume is the best one volume history of philosophy in English.

Three Types of Religious Philosophy, Gordon H. Clark $6.95
In this book on apologetics, Clark examines empiricism, rational-

ism, dogmatism, and contemporary irrationalism, which does not rise to the level of philosophy. He offers a solution to the question, "How can Christianity be defended before the world?"

Works of Theology

The Atonement, Gordon H. Clark $8.95
This is a major addition to Clark's multi-volume systematic theology. In The Atonement, *Clark discusses the Covenants, the Virgin Birth and Incarnation, federal headship and representation, the relationship between God's sovereignty and justice, and much more. He analyzes traditional views of the Atonement and criticizes them in the light of Scripture alone.*

The Biblical Doctrine of Man, Gordon H. Clark $5.95
Is man soul and body or soul, spirit, and body? What is the image of God? Is Adam's sin imputed to his children? Is evolution true? Are men totally depraved? What is the heart? These are some to the questions discussed and answered from Scripture in this book.

Cornelius Van Til: The Man and The Myth $2.45
John W. Robbins
The actual teachings of this eminent Philadelphia theologian have been obscured by the myths that surround him. This book penetrates those myths and criticizes Van Til's surprisingly unorthodox views of God and the Bible.

Faith and Saving Faith, Gordon H. Clark $6.95
The views of the Roman Catholic church, John Calvin, Thomas Manton, John Owen, Charles Hodge, and B.B. Warfield are discussed in this book. Is the object of faith a person or a proposition? Is faith more than belief? Is belief more than thinking with assent, as Augustine said?

In a world chaotic with differing views of faith, Clark clearly explains the Biblical view of faith and saving faith.

God's Hammer: The Bible and Its Critics, Gordon H. Clark $6.95
    The starting point of Christianity, the doctrine on which all other doctrines depend, is "The Bible alone is the Word of God written, and therefore inerrant in the autographs." Over the centuries the opponents of Christianity, with Satanic shrewdness, have concentrated their attacks on the truthfulness and completeness of the Bible. In the twentieth century the attack is not so much in the fields of history and archaeology as in philosophy. Clark's brilliant defense of the complete truthfulness of the Bible is captured in this collection of eleven major essays.

The Incarnation, Gordon H. Clark $8.95
    Who was Christ? The attack on the Incarnation in the nineteenth and twentieth centuries has been vigorous, but the orthodox response has been lame. Clark reconstructs the doctrine of the Incarnation building upon and improving upon the Chalcedonian definition.

In Defense of Theology, Gordon H. Clark $12.95
    There are four groups to whom Clark addresses this book: the average Christians who are uninterested in theology, the atheists and agnostics, the religious experientialists, and the serious Christians. The vindication of the knowledge of God against the objections of three of these groups is the first step in theology.

The Johannine Logos, Gordon H. Clark $5.95
    Clark analyzes the relationship between Christ, who is the truth, and the Bible, He explains why John used the same word to refer to both Christ and his teaching. Chapters deal with the Prologue to John's Gospel, Logos and Rheemata, Truth, and Saving Faith.

Logical Criticisms of Textual Criticism, Gordon H. Clark $2.95
    In this critique of the science of textual criticism, Dr. Clark exposes the fallacious argumentation of the modern textual critics and defends

the view that the early Christians knew better than the modern critics which manuscripts of the New Testament were more accurate.

Pat Robertson: A Warning to America, John W. Robbins $6.95
The Protestant Reformation was based on the Biblical principle that the Bible is the only revelation from God, yet a growing religious movement, led by Pat Robertson, asserts that God speaks to them directly. This book addresses the serious issue of religious fanaticism in America by examining the theological views of Pat Robertson.

Predestination, Gordon H. Clark $7.95
Clark thoroughly discusses one of the most controversial and pervasive doctrines of the Bible: that God is, quite literally, Almighty. Free will, the origin of evil, God's omniscience, creation, and the new birth are all presented within a Scriptural framework. The objections of those who do not believe in the Almighty God are considered and refuted. This edition also contains the text of the booklet, Predestination in the Old Testament.

Scripture Twisting in the Seminaries. Part 1: Feminism $5.95
John W. Robbins
An analysis of the views of three graduates of Westminster Seminary on the role of women in the church.

Today's Evangelism: Counterfeit or Genuine? $6.95
Gordon H. Clark
Clark compares the methods and messages of today's evangelists with Scripture, and finds that Christianity is on the wane because the Gospel has been distorted or lost. This is an extremely useful and enlightening book.

The Trinity, Gordon H. Clark $8.95
Apart from the doctrine of Scripture, no teaching of the Bible is more important than the doctrine of God. Clark's defense of the orthodox doctrine of the Trinity is a principal portion of a major new

work of Systematic Theology now in progress. There are chapters on the deity of Christ, Augustine, the incomprehensibility of God, Bavinck and Van Til, and the Holy Spirit, among others.

What Do Presbyterians Believe? Gordon H. Clark $7.95
    This classic introduction to Christian doctrine has been republished. It is the best commentary on the Westminster Confession of Faith that has ever been written.

Commentaries on the New Testament

Colossians, Gordon H. Clark $6.95
Ephesians, Gordon H. Clark $8.95
First and Second Thessalonians, Gordon H. Clark $5.95
The Pastoral Epistles (I and II Timothy and Titus) $9.95
    Gordon H. Clark
    All of Clark's commentaries are expository, not technical, and are written for the Christian layman. His purpose is to explain the text clearly and accurately so that the Word of God will be thoroughly known by every Christian. Revivals of Christianity come only through the spread of God's truth. The sound exposition of the Bible, through preaching and through commentaries on Scripture, is the only method of spreading that truth.

The Trinity Library

    We will send you one copy of each of the 31 books listed above for the low price of $150. The regular price of these books is $226. Or you may order the books you want individually on the order blank on the next page. Because some of the books are in short supply, we must reserve the right to substitute others of equal or greater value in The Trinity Library.
    Thank you for your attention. We hope to hear from you soon. This special offer expires June 30, 1992.

Order Form

Name _____

Address _____

_____

Please: ☐ add my name to the mailing list for *The Trinity Review*. I
            understand that there is no charge for the *Review*.

          ☐ accept my tax deductible contribution of $ _____
            for the work of the Foundation.

          ☐ send me _____ copies of *Today's Evangelism: Coun-
            terfeit or Genuine?* I enclose as payment
            $ _____.

          ☐ send me the Trinity Library of 31 books. I enclose $150 as
            full payment for it.

          ☐ send me the following books. I enclose full payment in the
            amount of $ _____ for them.

_____

_____

_____

_____

_____

_____

_____

Mail to: The Trinity Foundation
                  Post Office Box 700
                  Jefferson, MD 21755

Please add $1.00 for postage on orders less than $10. Thank you.
For quantity discounts, please write to the Foundation.

Supralapsarianism –
    extreme Calvinistic
position